TEACHER'S BOOK

Rising St

An Intermediate Course

Luke Prodromou

MACMILLAN

Macmillan Education
Between Towns Road, Oxford OX4 3PP
A division of Macmillan Publishers Limited
Companies and representatives throughout the world

ISBN 0 333 95346 0

Text © Luke Prodromou 2001

Design and illustration © Macmillan Publishers Limited 2001

Heinemann is a trademark of Harcourt Education, used under licence

First published 2001

Designed by jameslewis@xen

Typeset by Don Dolby

Illustrated by Val Saunders

Cover design by Pentacor

Printed in Thailand

2009 2008 2007 2006 2005
17 16 15 14 13 12 11 10 9 8

Contents

Reading	Listening	Speaking	Writing
'Life at the top' • Multiple matching	Interview with a girl rock group • Blank filling	• Pairwork interview (Could you be famous?)	• Letter of application (for a job)
'Youth culture' • Note taking	Four speakers talking about clothes • Multiple matching	• Pairwork interview (life last year)	• Informal letter (describing a party)
'Where it's at' • Multiple choice	Three speakers talking about different countries • True/False	• Describing photos (cities)	• Letter of complaint (to a language school)
'Magic circles' • Gapped text	Interview with a magician • Multiple choice	• Describing photos (magic)	• Short story (describing a show)
'Boys will be boys' • Multiple matching	Talking about falling in love • Blank filling	• Pairwork interview (favourite things)	• Article (friendship)
'A star is born' • Multiple matching (headings)	Interview with an astronomer • True/False	• Discussion (future plans)	• E-mail (describing a school trip)
'Earthquake!' • Multiple choice	Four speakers talking about environmental issues • Multiple matching	• Information gap (what to do during a fire)	• Leaflet (environmental advice)
'Why playing is important for kids' • Gapped text	Discussion about school breaks and holidays • True/False	• Pairwork task (planning a school curriculum)	• Article (a perfect day)
'Humour is an international language' • Gapped text	Four speakers describing embarrassing moments • Multiple matching	• Information gap (jokes) • Describing pictures	• Short story (an embarrassing day)
'Jungle boy' • Multiple matching (headings)	Talk show about being left-handed • Blank filling	• Information gap (spot the difference)	• Project (an ancient civilization)
'Nobel women' • Multiple matching	Interview about Amnesty International • Blank filling	• Pairwork task (discussing human rights)	• Article (a person you admire)
'Almost human?' • Multiple choice	Interview with a futurologist • True/False	• Discussion (life in the future)	• E-mail (future plans)
'Their names were Bond' • Multiple matching	Extract from a 'Charles Pond' film • Blank filling	• Describing photos & discussion (violence in the media)	• Short adventure story
'A meeting with Picasso' • Multiple matching (headings)	Interview with a photographer • Blank filling	• Describing a painting	• Description (of a painting)
'Monarch without a kingdom' • Gapped text	Four speakers talking about animals • Multiple matching	• Pairwork task (planning a trip to the zoo) • Information gap (eagles quiz)	• Letter asking for information (about a holiday)

Introduction

Description of the course

Shining Star is an intermediate course aimed at teenage learners. It consists of fifteen units of six pages. Each unit should take about four hours. There are also five review units. The course provides approximately 70 hours of teaching time. In addition to this, teachers should allow time in class for checking work done from the Practice Book and for conducting tests.

All units in the Student's Book contain the same sections in the same order, thus providing systematic coverage of grammar, vocabulary and language skills. Each unit begins with a reading text and focuses on a particular area of grammar. Each unit has a listening text and two vocabulary sections. Students are given the opportunity to put both grammar and vocabulary into practice in speaking activities related to the themes and language of the unit. Each unit ends with writing activities, which are given special attention in *Shining Star*.

Components of the course

The course consists of

- A Student's Book containing all the core material, a writing reference section, a grammar reference section and phrasal verb dictionary

- A Practice Book containing extra exercises to be used either in class or as homework assignments. They give extra practice of the grammar and vocabulary taught in the Student's Book. At the end of each unit there is a section called 'Develop your English'. These sections revise basic language which may not have appeared in the unit and extend students' vocabulary through word formation exercises.

- A photocopiable Test Booklet containing one progress test for each unit; three end-of-term tests and one end-of-year test.

- A Teacher's Book containing teacher's notes for each unit, suggestions for optional activities and early finishers, answers to all the exercises in the Student's Book, answer keys to the Practice Book and Test Booklet and photocopiable extra writing activities with a correction code table.

- A cassette tape containing all the listening material, including songs

Structure of the course

Background information about British, American and global culture is provided, where necessary, in starred text notes at the beginning of the section concerned in the Teacher's Book. These notes should be read by the teacher before the lesson and used to answer any queries students may have about the texts.

The fifteen units are structured as follows:

1 Reading

Each unit introduces the overall topic by means of photographs and other visuals. These are followed by a reading text which also provides a context for much of the grammar and vocabulary to be practised in that unit. The texts have been adapted from authentic sources and have been chosen to appeal to teenage learners with local and global interests.

The reading section provides material for a whole lesson, practising the skills involved in reading comprehension and the grammar and vocabulary from the text.

The approach to reading is one that develops comprehension rather than just testing it and can be divided into three stages: pre-reading, while reading and after reading.

• a pre-reading task sets the context and encourages purposeful reading. This is done in various ways: by getting students to talk about the topic using the visuals or written statements; getting students to predict from the pictures or other prompts; getting students to work on relevant vocabulary. On the whole, this pre-reading phase draws on students' background knowledge and experience and any previous language relevant to the task. The idea is to facilitate the reading process – to graft new information on what the students already know.

• while reading – this takes the form of questions, such as 'read the text and check your predictions/guesses'; 'read the text and answer the questions/complete the chart', etc. This phase of the reading process encourages various kinds of reading

- skimming to get the general idea

- scanning for a specific piece of information

- reading for detail

Students are encouraged to underline the section of text where they find the answers to comprehension questions. This helps them focus attention on the task and give specific feedback, using the line numbers at the side of the texts. Underlining also helps the teacher monitor whether the students have actually completed the task and the correct line reference are given in the answer boxes in the teacher's notes.

• after reading – this task may be either in the Student's Book or the teacher's notes and asks the students to reflect briefly on what they have read and to react in some way – by expressing their opinion on the subject, agreeing or disagreeing with something in the text, reading between the lines and so on. This phase of the reading process aims to fix the topic and the language of the text in the students' memory by introducing an element of personalization and active involvement.

2 Vocabulary

From intermediate level upwards, vocabulary is a major area of language expansion. Vocabulary 1, which follows immediately after the reading text, focuses on words from the text which may cause students difficulties. The task may focus, for example, on words with a similar or contrasting meaning. The Teacher's Book often provides additional vocabulary items to be checked or additional illustrative contexts for some of the words. Teachers will also find useful concept questions to help check students' understanding of vocabulary. Students are usually asked to underline the part of the text which contains the vocabulary in question. This will help them find items later for revision purposes.

Vocabulary 2, which appears on the fifth page of each unit, focuses on specific aspects of vocabulary building such as topic areas, word formation, synonyms, opposites, compound nouns, words of related meaning, word families and idioms. The aim is to expand students' knowledge of the English vocabulary system.

3 Grammar

There are two grammar sections in each unit. Grammar 1 follows the reading text and words from the text. Grammar 2 usually follows the listening or speaking activity. The grammar is based on the need to revise and develop the structures appropriate to intermediate level. It is assumed the students will have covered basic aspects of grammar (tenses, word order, interrogatives, etc) but need to expand and add new items to their grammatical repertoire (conditionals, modal verbs and uses of the future). The grammar presentation draws on the reading text for examples in context. Students are often asked to search the text for examples of the target grammar. This acts as useful revision of the text and an illustration of how the language works.

The grammar box presents the basic form, meaning and use of the grammar. For more detailed information, students may refer to the grammar reference section at the back of the Student's Book. The grammar box can be used to help students check what they may already know. Tips for using the grammar boxes, beyond just reading them aloud, are given in the teacher's notes.

After the grammar box there is usually practice of the grammar at sentence level and in context. Both are useful ways of reinforcing understanding of the grammar – sentence level exercises help students focus on the form and basic meaning of the structure while context exercises focus on the use of the structure.

4 Speaking

The speaking tasks usually follow Grammar 1 and appear on the third or fourth page of each unit. The speaking tasks are often an extension of the topic dealt with either in the reading text or the listening text. The themed sections are designed to help students by giving them familiar material to talk about.

The basic approach to speaking is to make the task practical for a class of teenage students. This means

- making the topic relevant to their interests
- providing appropriate forms of guidance
- providing a reason for speaking

The topics match the range of experience one would expect at this age: hobbies and interests; music; leisure; travel; studying and so on. The guidance so essential to successful speaking at this level takes the form of pictures, useful words and phrases and topics to talk about. Some tasks are information-gap activities, which encourage communication by giving pairs of students different sets of information. This information will be found on the communicative activities pages at the back of the Student's Book.

5 Listening

The listening activities aim to teach as well as to test comprehension. Their topics are often related to the topics in the reading texts and speaking tasks. Students are asked to complete notes, put verbal or visual information in the correct categories, answer true or false questions, multiple choice and so on. The aim is to provide a variety of reasons for listening (developing listening skills follows a parallel process to that of developing reading skills). Students listen

- to get the gist of the text (global listening)
- to find a specific piece of information
- to find detail

As with reading, this range of skills reflects what we do in real life. The cassette provides students with a range of contexts, accents and styles that reflects the way English is spoken in the world today. Teachers can make listening texts easier (in mixed-level classes) by reading parts, then using the cassette to make the task more natural and to increase the level of difficulty.

6 Writing

As with reading, the writing activities develop rather than test existing skills. Pre-writing tasks analyse and revise appropriate vocabulary and structures with the help of a model letter, article, story, etc. Each model also serves to illustrate the way a text is organized into topics and paragraphs. A writing reference section at the back of the Student's Book gives a summary and profile of the main features of the eight types of writing task covered in the units. The accompanying photocopiable extra writing activities in the Teacher's Book provide further practice if needed. These three components together offer a complete and practical approach to the teaching of writing at this level.

1 Success!

Topics
Rich and successful young people, fame, pop groups, actors

Grammar
Present simple, present continuous, stative verbs

Vocabulary
Personality, negative adjective prefixes, noun suffixes

Reading
'Life at the top': multiple matching

Listening
Interview with a girl rock group: blank filling

Speaking
Pairwork interview (Could you be famous?)

Writing
Transactional letter (application for a job)

Reading (pages 4–5)

☆ Text notes

• Tara Lipinski is a 15-year-old ice-skater and millionaire. She appears in adverts and on talk shows.

• Liz Evans is a 17-year-old model. She earns a lot of money modelling.

• Ramit Bharti Mittal is the 18-year-old son of a millionaire. He lives in Delhi and spends a lot of his father's money.

• The Campbell Food Company is a large American food company famous for its soup.

• A Chevrolet is a large, American, family car, also known as a Chevy.

• Birmingham is the second biggest city in Britain. It is a well-known industrial centre in the middle of England.

• Designer clothes are designed and made by famous design houses such as Versace and Armani. People who wear designer clothes are very wealthy.

• BMW is a well-known German car manufacturer who make expensive executive and sports cars. People who drive BMWs are wealthy. The cars are a status symbol. Even owning a BMW motorcycle would be prestigious.

1

• Establish the topic of the text by asking students to work in pairs, look at the photographs and answer the question. Elicit ideas from the class.

• Students read the texts quickly (skim) and match each one to the correct photo. Feedback.

• Write these key words on the board: *rich, famous, successful*. Elicit from the students examples of people who became rich, famous and successful when they were young.

• Ask students to think about the advantages and disadvantages of becoming successful and famous when you are very young. Feedback, making sure that both the advantages and disadvantages are discussed.

• Students read the texts quickly again and compare the points made with their ideas.

2

• This is a scanning exercise. Students will need to look for specific information in each text. They do not need to worry about any other details or difficult vocabulary at this stage.

• Students read the texts again and match the information with the correct person A, B or C. Feedback, encouraging students to make reference to specific points in the text.

Answers
1 A (line 1)
2 C (lines 37–38))
3 B (line 18)
4 A (line 14)
5 B (line 29)
6 C (lines 40–41)
7 C (line 47)

3

• Students read the definitions. In pairs, students try to guess the words. Students check their guesses by reading the texts again, underlining the answers and writing them next to the correct definition. Feedback with reference to the texts.

Optional activity

• Students discuss these questions either in pairs or as a class:

Which of these people would you like as a friend? Why?

How would your life change if you were famous?

Grammar 1   (page 5)

Present simple, present continuous

Presentation: put the following sentences from the reading texts on the board and ask the students what tenses are used and why:

She appears in adverts (present simple, repeated action).

This 17-year-old is beginning to enjoy spending money (present continuous, change taking place at the present time).

Grammar boxes

Direct students to the grammar boxes on page 5. Go through the grammar boxes with the students or ask them to read them silently and ask you anything they do not understand.

1

• Ask students to read text C again and underline other examples of the present simple and present continuous. Ask what uses they have/meanings they express. Feedback.

• Elicit from students what other uses/meanings of the present simple and present continuous they know.

2

• Students do the exercise either individually or as a class. Feedback, referring to the grammar boxes to

explain any difficulties. Ask students to justify their answers by referring to the explanations in the grammar boxes.

3

• Write these questions on the board and ask students to tell you what tense each one is in and why:

What's your name? (present simple, fact)

Where do you come from? (present simple, fact)

What are we learning at the moment? (present continuous, temporary present situation)

• Students do the exercise individually, in pairs or as a class. Feedback by asking one student to ask each question and another student to answer it.

4

• Students work in pairs asking each other the questions in exercise 3. They should give their own answers. This is a good opportunity for students to get to know each other. Direct their attention to the grammar boxes as a reminder of how to use the present simple and present continuous.

Speaking   (page 6)

Warm up: students work in groups and discuss these questions:
Who would like to be famous? Why?
What kind of people become famous?

• Feedback, encouraging students to give reasons for their answers.

1

• Students read the questionnaire. Check they understand the questions. Point out the use of the auxiliary *do* in the interrogative.

• Students read the questionnaire again and answer the questions. They can make a note of their answers if they wish.

• Students work in pairs and interview each other, making a note of their partner's answers. Encourage them to give more than a *Yes* or *No* answer where appropriate.

Early finishers

• Ask early finishers to write more questions in the simple present on the same topic or to interview another student.

2

• Feedback, asking students to report back on their partner, for example: *Maria never tells her friends all the latest gossip about famous people.*

• In pairs, students discuss who in the class they think is most likely to become famous and why. Feedback, encouraging students to give reasons for their answer.

Optional activity

Students write a brief report on 'Could you be famous?' for homework using their partner's and their own answers to the questionnaire.

Vocabulary I (page 6)

Personality

Warm up: write these words and expressions on the board: *a gossip, a show off, aggressive, nervous, have common sense, dull, funny, easy-going.*

• Ask the students to describe how these types of people behave.

I

• Ask students to decide whether the words and expressions in the box are positive or negative characteristics.

• Students work in pairs and put the words and expressions into the correct column. Feedback.

Answers
Positive: have common sense, funny, be easy-going
Negative: be a gossip, be a show off, aggressive,
    dull, nervous

2

• Students work in pairs to match the words and expressions in exercise 1 with the definitions. Feedback.

Answers

1	nervous	5	aggressive
2	funny	6	be easy-going
3	be a show off	7	dull
4	be a gossip	8	have common sense

Negative adjective prefixes

3

• Write these words on the board: *tidy, accurate, possible.* Ask students to form the negative of the words using *un-, in-,* or *im-*.

• Students work in groups and brainstorm as many words as possible that begin with these prefixes. Point out that most of these have a negative meaning.

• Students make the adjectives in 1–8 negative by choosing the appropriate prefix. Feedback.

Answers

1	uninteresting	5	inexpensive
2	unambitious	6	impractical
3	unsuccessful	7	unusual
4	unprepared	8	inexperienced

4

• Students skim through the sentences. Make sure they understand them. Students work individually or as a class and replace the underlined words or phrases with a negative adjective from exercise 3. Feedback.

Answers

1 uninteresting
2 unprepared
3 inexpensive
4 unusual
5 impractical

Optional activity

• Ask students to choose positive adjectives to describe themselves. They may use other adjectives they know, in addition to those in exercises 1–3.

Listening (page 7)

Warm up: use the picture on page 7 to introduce the topic of all-girl pop groups. Ask students to work in groups and think of as many all-girl pop groups as they can. Encourage them to think about the kind of music they play, their age and nationality, and whether or not they enjoy being famous.

I

• Students look at the picture again and guess what kind of music Girlzone play. Encourage them to give reasons for their guesses.

2

• Explain that in preparation for the listening exercise, students are going to check the meaning of some words. Provide the following definitions for students to find a matching word:

to break something into little pieces (smash)
to shout when you want to show you like something (cheer)
to happen, occur (arise)

• Alternatively you could ask the students some check questions, for example:

What happens when you drop a glass on the floor? (It smashes.)
What do you do at a basketball match when your team wins? (You cheer.)

• Explain to students that they are going to listen to an interview with Girlzone to find the answers to the questions. Students read the questions. Make sure they understand them.

• Students listen to the tape for the answers to the questions. Feedback, encouraging them to give reasons for their answers.

Answers

1 No
2 Yes
3 No

3

• Explain that students are going to listen to the interview again but this time they will need to listen more carefully because they are going to complete some sentences with information from the tape. Give them some time to read the sentences. Make sure they understand them.

• Play the tape again, pausing at the points indicated in the tapescript to give students time to write down their answers. Feedback by asking students to read out the completed sentences.

Answers

1 very different 1970s bands
2 at a school talent contest
3 smashed her/the
4 first prize/£1,000/a day in the recording studio
5 their music teacher
6 home
7 a lift

Optional activity

• Students discuss these questions either in pairs or as a class:

Would you like to be a member of a group like Girlzone? What would you like/dislike about their lifestyle?

• Feedback, encouraging students to give reasons for their answers.

Tapescript (exercises 2 and 3)

INTERVIEWER: People often compare you with the Spice Girls – how do you feel about that?

BAND MEMBER 1: Oh dear, here we go again. We don't even like them. I mean, don't misunderstand me – we really respect them for what they've done. But their music just isn't anything we're interested in.

INTERVIEWER: What are your feelings about school?

BAND MEMBER 2: At school, we were all very different from the other girls because when all our friends liked the Spice Girls and Boyzone, <u>we were really keen on very different 1970s bands – you know, like T Rex.</u> **(Pause question 1)**

INTERVIEWER: How did it all begin?

BAND MEMBER 3: Well, you see, our parents played us videos from that time and we found those bands had something that's missing from music today. I think it was the fact that we all liked something different from everyone else at school that brought us together and made us start a band of our own.

INTERVIEWER: And when did you have your first success?

BAND MEMBER 4: Right, <u>it was at a school talent contest with lots of schools competing. That was when we first got noticed.</u> **(Pause question 2)**

INTERVIEWER: What did you do that was different from other people, do you think?

BAND MEMBER 4: We wanted to do something silly, but we didn't know what. I borrowed a guitar from someone who'd been playing and, as we were finishing, <u>I decided to smash it up.</u> (Pause question 3) The guy I borrowed the guitar from wasn't all that pleased, but everyone else was cheering. I'd only ever seen it done on TV, so I didn't realize how difficult it was. The crowd started counting each time I smashed the guitar against the stage: 'One … two … three …'. It took me thirteen attempts before I managed to break it.

INTERVIEWER: And you won the contest?

BAND MEMBER 1: Well, we were the only girl group taking part and we were much younger than everyone else who'd entered, <u>so they gave us first prize. We won a thousand pounds in the contest, but it all went to the school. We also won a day in the recording studio.</u> **(Pause question 4)**

INTERVIEWER: How did you become professional?

BAND MEMBER 2: <u>Our music teacher at school encouraged us to start taking the band seriously, and she helped us to make contacts.</u> (Pause question 5) It all led to us being given a contract by Simon Fuller, the former manager of the Spice Girls.

INTERVIEWER: How do you feel about your success?

BAND MEMBER 3: It's very exciting, of course, but there are disadvantages. <u>Homesickness is the worst part. We get home maybe once or twice a week. It becomes more of a lifestyle than a job. It's hard.</u>
(Pause question 6)

INTERVIEWER: Do you get on very well with each other?

BAND MEMBER 4: Well, problems arise because we spend a lot of time in each other's company. Kate's dad had to <u>separate us in the lift the other day because we were having a terrible row.</u> **(Pause question 7)** We don't pull each other's hair or kick each other, but we do quarrel.

Grammar 2 (page 7)

Stative verbs

Presentation: write these sentences on the board:

These flowers are smelling good.   *These flowers smell good*
I am loving ice-cream.   *I love ice-cream.*

• Ask students to tell you which sentences are correct. Elicit the reason why from the students. If students cannot tell you why, explain that there are some verbs which are only used in the present simple.

Grammar box

• Direct students to the grammar box on page 7. Ask students to choose one verb from each category and make an example sentence with each one.

• **Note:** some of these verbs, with a change of meaning, can also be used in the present continuous. Do not spend time on these distinctions at this stage.

I

• Students read the interview quickly. Ask them these check questions to make sure they understand:

Who is A? (interviewer)
Who is B? (famous person)
What kind of work does the famous person do? (TV)
How do we know the famous person is rich? (servant, horses)

•Students complete the interview in pairs. One student completes the A sentences and the other completes the B sentences. Students then compare answers and complete the dialogue together.

• Feedback by asking pairs of students to read the dialogue aloud.

Answers

1	do you start	7	like	14	is getting
2	have	8	prefer	15	understand
3	ask	9	do you own	16	are you
4	do you begin	10	have		recording
5	do you mean	11	ride		
6	Are you working	12	believe		
		13	feel		

Vocabulary 2 (page 8)

Noun suffixes

Warm up: write these definitions on the board and ask students to match them with adjectives in the box:

Someone who believes in their own ability (confident)
Someone who always asks questions and wants to fund out new things (curious)
Someone who always thinks things are bad and will be bad (pessimistic)

• **Note:** do not spend a lot of time talking about the meaning of these words. The focus is on the form of the adjectives and nouns. A quick explanation of unknown words is all that is required.

• Write *confident, shy, pessimistic* on the board. Elicit from the students which suffixes can be added to the adjectives to make nouns (confidence, shyness, pessimism). Point out the changes in spelling.

I

• Students change the adjectives to nouns by adding the appropriate suffix and making any necessary spelling changes. Feedback.

Answers

-ence: intelligence, confidence, impatience
-ness: stubbornness, shyness, politeness, friendliness, selfishness
-ism: pessimism
-ity: sensitivity, curiosity, popularity, generosity
-th: strength, warmth
-y: sympathy
-ion: attraction, competition
-no suffix: charm, energy, passion, success

2

☆ Text notes

The Chinese zodiac uses twelve animals to depict the signs of the zodiac, but they are different animals from the ones used in the western zodiac, with different meanings. The Chinese use pig, rabbit, bull, tiger, rat, dragon, snake, horse, goat, chicken, monkey and dog. Each sign says something about the personality of the person who is born under it.

• Ask students to work in groups and list the animals in the western zodiac. Ask them which sign they are and what this is supposed to say about their personality.

• Use the picture of the Chinese zodiac on page 8 to elicit from the students the animals used in the Chinese zodiac. Ask students to guess what each sign might say about personality of someone born under it.

• Students scan through the text to find animals and adjectives describing personality. Feedback.

animals: *tigers, rabbits, dragons, snakes, rams*
adjectives: *brave, optimistic, shy, generous, polite, tough*

• Students work individually to complete the text. Point out that they will have to think about which form of the word to use and change the spelling if necessary. Feedback.

Answers

1	different	5	actors	9	reputation
2	competition/competing	6	strength	10	sensitive
3	famous	7	confidence	11	sympathy
4	friendship	8	attractive		

Optional activity

• Students choose one of the famous people from the text and write a description using information from the text. Point out that they should not write the person's name in the description and that they can use adjectives other than those in the text.

• Students work in pairs and read their descriptions. They guess who their partner has written about and decide if that person is really like their Chinese zodiac sign.

Writing (pages 8–9)

Transactional letter (application for a job)

Warm up: explain to students that they are going to look at a letter written in response to an advert for young actors to take part in a movie, *The Young and the Beautiful*. Ask students to tell you what the movie might be about.

• Elicit from the students adjectives to describe this type of movie.

1

• Elicit from the students adjectives and nouns that could be used to describe a successful film star. Students write them under the correct heading.

• Students look through the unit for other adjectives and nouns which could be used to describe a successful film star. They add them to the list under the correct heading.

Suggested answers

Adjectives: sociable, popular, attractive, confident, charming, competitive, famous, passionate, funny, ambitious
Nouns: confidence, charm, energy, passion, warmth, ambition

2

• Ask students to read the advert on page 9 quickly and to list the adjectives and nouns that are used to describe the type of person the advert is looking for: *confident, sociable, fit, healthy, natural leader*

• Ask students to read the advert again. Ask them the following check questions to make sure they understand:

What do you have to do if you want to be in the movie?
(apply for an audition)
What do you have to do if you want to apply for an audition?
(send a letter and colour photograph)

• Ask students to read the letter of application on page 9 and to underline the words and phrases in the letter that match the adjectives and nouns they found in the advert. Feedback.

• Direct students to the diagram on page 9. Ask the following check questions:

How does paragraph 1/2/3 start? (1=I am writing, 2=First of all, 3=I hope)
Where is the salutation? (at the beginning)
Where is the closing paragraph? (at the end)

• Students read the letter again and complete the diagram individually or in pairs.

• Feedback, referring to the paragraph or section of the letter first and then the information. If you can, copy the diagram onto an overhead projector transparency and complete it with the students.

Answers

Salutation: Dear Sir or Madam
Paragraph 1, Reason for writing:
  1 interested in applying for an audition
  2 give more information
Tenses used:
  1 present continuous
  2 present simple
Paragraph 2, Achievments:
  1 school play
  2 of basketball team
  3 enjoys making decisions
Paragraph 3, Schoolwork:
  1 tests
  2 English, gymnastics
Closing:
  1 I look forward to hearing from you
  2 Yours faithfully

2 Talking about my generation

Topics
Youth culture, youth movements, appearance, hair, clothes, parties

Grammar
Past simple, past continuous

Vocabulary
Clothes, adjective opposites

Reading
'Youth culture': note taking

Listening
Four speakers talking about clothes: multiple matching

Speaking
Pairwork interview (life last year)

Writing
Informal letter (describing a party)

Reading (pages 10–12)

☆ Text notes

• The title of this unit comes from a famous song by the 1960s British rock group, The Who, 'My generation'. The song is about how young people feel misunderstood and put down by older generations.

• The hippy movement started in the 1960s. Men and women grew their hair long, wore Indian style clothes and usually wore or carried flowers. They believed in love and peace which became known as flower power. Hippies often lived in communes, were vegetarian and did not conform. Bob Dylan (1941-) is an American folk singer and songwriter. He became famous for writing protest songs in the 1960s the most famous of which was 'Blowin' in the Wind'. The Beatles were the most famous British pop group of all time.

• Punks appeared in the 1970s and were against money and consumerism. They listened to punk rock, which was loud, often violent, music. They wore black clothes, Doctor Marten Boots, put safety pins through their ears and noses and often had strange, spiky, multicoloured hairstyles. The Sex Pistols were one of the most famous punk rock groups of the 1970s. The two most well-known members of the group were Johnny Rotten and Sid Vicious.

• Ravers were young people in the 1980s and 1990s who enjoyed going to illegal and spontaneous parties in large empty buildings. A style of music developed called Techno Music and ravers danced all night to it. Acid music was popular in the 1990s. It was very loud electronic music and was accompanied by strange lighting effects.

Warm up: Establish the topic of the text by writing the names of these youth movements on the board: *Hippies*, *Punks* and *Ravers*.

• Ask students what they know about them. Elicit ideas about beliefs, clothes and music. Feedback making sure the clothes and music of each movement are discussed.

1

• Students read the texts quickly (skim) and match each one to the correct photo. Feedback.

Answers
A 2
B 3
C 1

2

• Students read the texts again (scan) for the information needed to complete the chart. They should not worry about difficult words at this stage. Set a time limit of ten minutes for this.

Answers
Hippies: 1960s and 1970s/Indian-style silk dresses/Bob Dylan, The Beatles
Punks: 1970s/ripped T-shirts, Doc Marten boots, leather jackets/Sex Pistols
Ravers: 1980s/loose T-shirts, jeans/acid and techno

Optional activity

• Students work in groups and decide which of the youth movements they would have liked to belong to. Feedback, encouraging them to give reasons for their answers.

3

• Students read the words.

• Write these definitions on the board. Students match them with the correct word.

when something very special happens (exciting)

very loud (noisy)

very smart (formal)

to like something or someone a lot (love)

not special (ordinary)

no more room inside (full)

• In pairs, students try to guess the opposites. Students check their guesses by reading the texts again, underlining the answers and writing them next to the correct word. Feedback with reference to the text.

Answers

1 unusual (line 2)
2 quiet (line 5)
3 hate (line 21)
4 boring (line 22)
5 empty (line 30)
6 casual (line 31)

Grammar 1 (page 11)

Past simple

Presentation: ask students to skim the texts and tell you which tense is used most. Elicit why from the students (past simple, completed actions at definite time in past).

Grammar box

• Direct students to the grammar box on page 11. Ask them to underline the past simple verbs in the example sentences. Feedback.

• Make sure students understand the uses of the past simple.

1

• Students work individually to find and underline examples of the past simple in text A. Students check their answers in pairs. Feedback.

Answers

was, opposed, wore, had, lived, believed, went, started, showed, listened, enjoyed, wrote

Optional activities

• Ask students to divide the verbs into regular and irregular verbs.

• Elicit the uses of the past simple in text A.

2

• Ask students to read the headline of the text on page 11. Elicit what they think it is about.

• Write these definitions on the board and ask students to read the text on page 11 quickly to find the words to match them:

long thin points (spikes)

jewellery worn in ears (earrings)

worn round the neck, on a shirt or by a priest (collar)

a strip of cloth or leather worn round the arms, legs or head (band)

a small piece of metal worn on boots, belts or in this case in the nose (stud)

• Students work in pairs and describe the picture. Feedback.

• Students read the text again to find the mistake in the picture. They should not worry about the missing words at this stage.

Answer

green hair should be black

3

• Students work in pairs and complete the text with the past simple form of the verbs in brackets. Feedback.

Answers

1 fired   6 dismissed
2 said   7 began
3 were   8 felt
4 included   9 said
5 warned   10 denied

Early finishers

• Ask students which past simple forms are regular (fired, included, warned, dismissed, denied) and which are irregular (all the rest).

4

• Direct students to the example and focus on the use of the auxiliary *did* (with main verbs when we form questions and negatives).

• Students work in pairs to form questions in the past simple using the notes given.

- Students work in pairs to find the answers to the questions from the text.

- Feedback by asking one student to ask the question and another to answer it.

Answers

1 What things did he wear? (He wore 18 earrings, a metal collar, steel bands and a stud through his nose.)
2 When did he begin to wear spikes? (He began to wear spikes last June.)
3 What did Peter put on his hair? (He put glue on it.)
4 Why were the spikes dangerous? (Because someone could be injured by standing near Peter.)
5 What problem did Peter have? (Sleeping.)

Optional activity

- In groups, students discuss who they think was right, Peter or Rolls Royce. Feedback, encouraging students to give reasons for their answers.

Speaking (page 12)

Warm up: elicit from students how to form *yes/no* questions in the past simple (with *did*).

- Students work in groups and write down four *yes/no* questions in the past simple to find out what you did yesterday. Monitor to make sure that the questions start with *Did you ... ?*

- Students ask you their questions.

- Write your short answers on the board: *Yes I did/No I didn't.* Point out that we use the auxiliary *did* in these short answers, too.

1

- Explain that students are going to interview their partner to find out what they did last year. Make sure students understand the activity by directing their attention to the example and asking a student to answer the question.

- Students ask and answer the questions in pairs, making a note of their partner's answers.

- Feedback by asking pairs to conduct their interviews in front of the class. Focus on the correct use of the auxiliary *did*.

2

- Explain that students are now going to find out more information about what their partner did last year by asking *wh-* questions and questions with *How/How long*.

- Direct students to the example questions, focusing on the use of the auxiliary *did*. Elicit other questions they could use.

- Students ask and answer questions to find out more information about what their partner did last year, making a note of their partner's answers. Feedback by asking pairs to conduct their interviews in front of the class.

Optional activity

- Students write a paragraph about what their partner did last year using the answers to the questions.

Vocabulary 1 (page 12)

Clothes

Warm up: students work in pairs and write down as many items of clothing as they can. They can look at what other students are wearing for ideas. Feedback.

1

- Make sure students know the clothing items in the box by asking some check questions:
Who wears a shirt and tie?
Where does a tie go?
Would you wear a jumper in July?
Is a suit formal or informal?

- Use similar questions for the remaining items.

- Direct students to the photographs on page 12. Students work in pairs and describe the clothes in each photograph. Feedback.

Answers

A hat, skirt, short-sleeved shirt
B shirt and tie, suit, jacket
C school uniform, shirt and tie, jumper
D overalls, dressing gown

2

- The aim of this exercise is to activate vocabulary for describing clothes. Elicit some examples before asking students to write sentences in their vocabulary notebooks.

- **Note:** It is a good idea for all students to have a separate vocabulary notebook, divided into topic areas. The sentences they write in this task will go in the *Clothes* section of their vocabulary notebook.

Early finishers

- Students write about what other members of their family wore on the same occasions.

(page 12)

Warm up: In groups, students write down as many jobs as they can. Feedback, eliciting from students what the people who do the jobs wear.

1

• Students look at the photographs and identify the occupations.

Answers	
a police officer	c schoolboy
b TV announcer	d nurse

2 🎧

• Explain that students will hear each person in the photos talking about their job.

• Students listen and match each speaker with a photo. Feedback with reference to the tape.

Answers

Speaker 1: c	Speaker 3: d
Speaker 2: a	Speaker 4: b

3 🎧

• Students read the questions. Make sure they understand them.

• Students listen again and match the speakers with the questions. Point out that students have to write the number of the speaker (1–4) next to the question. Feedback with reference to the tape.

Answers

A Speaker 4 (the colours have to match)
B Speaker 3 (I liked the idea of wearing a uniform)
C Speaker 1 (you should be allowed to show your individuality)
D Speaker 2 (in the summer we're allowed to wear a short-sleeved shirt)
E Speaker 3 (since we're badly paid)

Optional activity

• Ask students to work in groups and discuss the advantages and disadvantages of wearing school uniforms.

Tapescript (exercises 2 and 3)

SPEAKER 1

I hate having to <u>wear a school uniform. I think you should be allowed to show your individuality, and clothes are something very personal.</u> **(question 3, C)** I don't see why everyone should look the same. After all, when you go to a party everyone's an individual, everyone's different. I went to a birthday party at my friend's house the other day and I just wore a pair of jeans and a T-shirt – oh, and a new pair of trainers –

and I felt great, I felt comfortable. Everyone else was wearing casual clothes too – you know, nothing very smart. But then, I suppose the trainers were quite expensive.

SPEAKER 2

There's no way I could avoid wearing a uniform in my job. <u>In the summer, we're allowed to wear a short-sleeved shirt</u> **(question 3, D)** but that's all. So, whether I'm directing the traffic or guarding an important building, I have to wear my uniform. People need to know who you are because they ask questions. Yesterday I was walking down the High Street when a tourist from Italy came up to me and asked the way to the post office. And the day before yesterday, a young girl ran up to me in a panic because she'd lost her purse. In situations like these, if I'm not wearing a uniform I can't do my job properly.

SPEAKER 3

In my job, it's important not only to *look* clean but to *be* clean – it's a matter of hygiene. When you're dealing with patients who may have serious diseases, everything has to be very clean. Most of us have to wear a uniform – I think it's comforting for the sick, especially the old and young children. I actually took up this particular profession partly <u>because I liked the idea of wearing a uniform</u>. **(question 3, B)** It makes me feel very proud. And that makes me feel a bit better, since <u>we're badly paid</u>. **(question 3, E)**

SPEAKER 4

When the whole country's looking at you, then <u>you've got to be very careful about your appearance</u>, haven't you? <u>The colours have to match and you have to look smart</u>, **(question 3, A)** but of course you mustn't go too far. Once, I remember, I was wearing a bright blue, flowery dress and my producer told me later that it was impossible to concentrate on what I was saying – the news just got lost in all the colours!

Oh, and I also go to the hairdresser's twice a week. On one occasion the programme was just starting when I realized I hadn't brushed my hair properly – I got a message through my earphones to tidy my hair!

Grammar 2 (page 13)

Past continuous
Grammar box

Direct students to the grammar box on page 13.

• Students read the three sentences and identify the past simple and past continuous in each one.

• Point out the example that uses both tenses. Elicit more examples from the students.

• Point out the difference between the completed actions of the past simple and the uses of the past continuous.

1

• Explain to students that the sentences are taken from the listening text. Students work individually to complete the three sentences. Feedback, eliciting why students chose each form.

Answers

1 was walking/asked   3 was just starting/realized
2 was wearing

2

• Students read the sentences.

• Explain that some of the sentences contain grammatical mistakes. Some are correct.

• Students work in pairs to find and correct the mistakes. Feedback, encouraging students to give reasons for their answers.

Answers

1 When I got to school
2 Correct
3 I was watching
4 The teacher was not there
5 Correct
6 Mark was riding his bike up a hill when he saw

3

• Establish the topic of the text using the photographs on page 13. Ask students where they think the photographs were taken.

• In pairs, students describe each photograph using the past simple and the past continuous. Feedback.

• Students skim through the text to find out which photograph it describes. Feedback with reference to the text.

Answers

photograph b

4

• Students work in pairs to complete the text. Remind them that they are focusing on the past simple and the past continuous. Feedback, encouraging students to give reasons for their answers.

Answers

1 were camping   8 were playing
2 was   9 arrived
3 was shining   10 were taking
4 was wearing   11 took
5 was not wearing 12 was jumping
6 felt   13 managed
7 went

Vocabulary 2 (page 14)

Adjective opposites

Warm up: as a fun activity ask students to think of an adjective. Go round the class. The first student says an adjective and the student next to them says the opposite of it. That student then says an adjective and so on.

1

• Point out that the adjectives in this exercise are based on the vocabulary in this unit.

• Students quickly look at the adjectives in both lists. Make sure they understand them.

• Students match the adjectives in list A with their opposites in list B. Feedback.

Answers

1 f   5 g
2 c   6 d
3 a   7 b
4 h   8 e

2

• Write the headings on the board. In groups, students brainstorm adjectives to go under each heading. They should not use adjectives from exercise 1. Feedback, writing their ideas under the headings.

• Students work individually or in pairs to add the adjectives from exercise 1 to the lists. Point out that some words can go in more than one group. Feedback.

• Students add the lists to their vocabulary notebooks.

Answers

Clothes: formal, casual, large, small, short, expensive, cheap, neat, untidy
People: formal, quiet, noisy, clever, stupid, serious, amusing, large, small, tall, short, neat, untidy
Party: formal, quiet, noisy, large, small, expensive, cheap

Early finishers

• Ask early finishers to write example sentences using the adjectives in exercises 1 and 2.

Writing (pages 14–15)

Informal letter

Warm up: explain that in this section the students are going to write an informal letter.

• Introduce the idea of an informal letter by writing the following on the board. Ask students which phrases are appropriate for a letter to a friend and which are better for a letter to a stranger:

Dear Madam/Dear Maria/I'm just writing to say/I am writing to apply for./I look forward to receiving your reply/Write soon/Yours sincerely/Best wishes/Love

• Elicit that in an informal letter first names should be used and that the close should be friendly and informal.

1

• Ask students to look at the photographs on page 14 and guess what the letter they are going to write will be about (a party of some kind, it could be a wedding reception/a birthday party).

• Students discuss the questions in pairs or as a class. Feedback.

Answers
1 a shows a birthday party, b shows a wedding
2 a – casual clothes/informal clothes
  b – formal clothes
3 a – blowing out candles on a cake
  b – having photos taken
4 Students' own answers

2

• Direct students to the model letter on page 15.

• Students read the letter and answer the questions. Feedback.

Answers
1 End-of-exams party
2 It was at a local disco, *Black and Red*
3 About 60
4 At one o'clock in the morning

3

• This exercise focuses on the language of an informal letter.

• Students read the letter again and underline the words and phrases. Feedback.

Answers
1 went on, sat around, put on, got up
2 was, wanted, held, decided, started, went on, sat, drank, put, got up, danced, left
3 was wearing, was drinking, was chatting
4 so, who, and, at first, after a while

• Elicit whether students think the letter is formal or informal.

• Ask students which words and phrases make the letter informal.

4

• Explain that students are going to write their own letter. Explain that the letter on page 15 is a model letter and ask students to read it again.

• Students work in pairs and choose a party they have been to. Explain that in answering questions 1–5, they will develop the content of their letter.

• Students make a note of their answers.

• Direct students to the model letter again. In pairs, they organize their notes into paragraphs using the notes on the letter as a guide. Monitor and help students make their paragraph plan if necessary.

5

• Assign the letter for homework. Students use their paragraph plan to organize their letter. Remind students to use informal language, the vocabulary in this unit and the model letter as a guide.

• In the next lesson students exchange and read letters making any necessary corrections or changes.

• Mark the letters. Set a time limit in another lesson to give feedback.

Sample letter (162 words)

Dear Debbie,

Thanks for writing. It was lovely to hear from you. I promised to write to you about Rosie's birthday party. OK, I'll do my best.

The party was at Rosie's flat (her parents were out). There were at least 25 people there.

Most of the kids, who were from our school, were wearing jeans and T-shirts. It was all very casual, of course. Tricia was different as always. She was wearing a long silky Indian dress. People brought flowers, there was lots to eat and lots of different kinds of music to dance to.

At first, everyone just stood around chatting and eating the food but then someone told a really good joke and everyone started laughing. Then Rosie put on some loud techno music and people started to dance and have a good time.

At about midnight, Rosie's parents came back and people started to leave. But it was a really great party.

That's all for now.

Write soon,

3 Around the world

Topics
Pop music centres in Britain, tourist destinations in Europe, Asia and Latin America

Grammar
Present perfect simple, present perfect continuous

Vocabulary
Compound nouns, travel

Reading
'Where it's at': multiple choice

Listening
Three speakers talking about different countries: true/false

Speaking
Describing photos (cities)

Writing
Transactional letter (complaint to a language school)

Reading (pages 16–17)

☆ Text notes

• Liverpool, an industrial port town in northwest England, was made famous by the Beatles and other pop groups in the 1960s. The River Mersey runs through the city which is why the music that came out of Liverpool in the 1960s was called the Mersey sound.

• Manchester is a big industrial city in northwest England. Oasis are a rock band from Manchester. They were extremely popular in the late 1990s.

• Bristol, an industrial port town in southwest England is home of trip hop, a popular rock movement of the 1990s. Massive Attack is a British rock band from Bristol formed in 1987. Their music mixes soul, hiphop, reggae, and rock.

• Memphis, Tennessee, on the Mississippi River, is the biggest city in the state, and is often associated with pop music, especially that of Elvis Presley (1935-1977), the most famous rock and roll singer of all time. Born in Tupelo Mississippi, he lived mostly in Memphis.

• Dublin is the capital of Ireland and centre of Irish folk music. Well-known bands from Dublin are U2 and the Chieftains. U2 are known for their political songs.

• Hiphop is a kind of American rock music with a heavy beat and special musical effects. It is often associated with graffiti art and breakdance.

Warm up: use the photos on page 16 to establish the topic of the text. Students look at the photos and see if they can name any of the people in them. Ask students what they know about them. Feedback.

Answers
Massive Attack – Bristol trip hop band
Portishead – Bristol band
Tricky – Bristol DJ, musician and record producer

1

• Students work in pairs to match the names in list A with the cities in list B.

• Students read the text quickly(skim) to check their answers.

Answers
1 c
2 a
3 d
4 b

2

• Students read the beginning of each statement (not the possible endings) and find and underline the part of the text that it refers to.

• This is a scanning exercise, which requires students to read the text quickly for specific information. Set a time limit of five minutes for this. Feedback with reference to the text and bear in mind that this exercise is not a test of general knowledge but a reading task. They should not worry about difficult words at this stage.

Answers
1	lines 3–8	4	lines 28–30
2	lines 9–10	5	lines 31–35
3	lines 22–23		

• Students read the possible endings for each statement, check back to where they found the beginning of each one, read around that point and choose the best answer. Warn them that they should not expect the wording of the text to be the same as that of the answer, but that the meaning should be the same. Feedback, with reference to the text.

3

• Students read the definitions. Make sure they understand them. Students should try and guess the word or phrase by reading the definition carefully before checking with the text. This encourages them to take a more active, independent approach to vocabulary.

• Point out that the paragraph where they can find the word is given. Students read the text again and find the words or phrases which have a similar meaning to the definitions. Feedback, with reference to the text.

Grammar 1 (page 17)

Present perfect simple

Presentation: ask students how many ways they know of talking about the past in English. Put some of their examples on the board. Briefly discuss the differences in meaning of the forms they have offered.

Grammar box

• Direct students to the grammar box on page 17 and ask them to read the three example sentences.

• Elicit from students the differences in meaning of the past simple and present perfect simple.

1

• Students find and underline examples of the present perfect simple in paragraph 2 of the text on page 16. Feedback, encouraging students to think about why each one is being used.

• Point out that we often follow the present perfect simple with the past simple, which gives more specific information about the event mentioned in the present perfect.

2

⭐ Text note

• Corfu is a Greek island in the Ionian sea. It is also known as Kerkyra. In the English speaking world it was made famous by the novelist Gerald Durrell in his novel *My Family and Other Animals*.

• Students complete the text, individually or in pairs. Feedback, encouraging students to give reasons for their answers.

3

• Ask students to look at the grammar box again. Elicit examples of the present perfect simple with the adverbs *just, yet, already, still, ever, never.*

• Students complete the sentences using the adverbs given. Feedback, encouraging students to give reasons for their answers.

Speaking (page 18)

Warm up: direct students to the photographs on page 18 and ask if they know anything about the two cities shown in the photographs. Students brainstorm what they know in groups.

1

• Explain that in this exercise, students are going to compare the photographs, using the expressions in the box. Use these check questions to make sure they understand them:
What do we call the front part of a picture? (the foreground)
What do we call the back part of a picture? (the background)
What is another word for centre? (middle)
What do we call a very tall building? (a skyscraper)
What are the boats called in Venice? (gondolas)

• Give students time to make a note of phrases/other words they might use to compare the photographs.

• Students work in pairs and compare the two photographs. Feedback.

Early finishers

• Ask early finishers to write down their comparison of the two photographs.

Optional activity

• In groups, students discuss which city they would prefer to live in and why.

Vocabulary 1 (page 18)

Compound nouns

Warm up: write these nouns on the board and ask students what they have in common:
postman, policewoman, doorbell, light switch, computer program, pen-friend
(They are all examples of compound nouns.)

• Elicit how these compound nouns are formed. Point out that not all compound nouns are made up of two nouns, but that the focus of this exercise is noun + noun.

• Point out that a compound noun can be written as one word, two words or with a hyphen. If in doubt, students should check with their dictionary.

• Elicit from students more examples of noun + noun compounds.

1

• Students match the nouns in list A with nouns in list B to make compounds. Feedback. Do not ask students for the meanings at this stage.

Answers
1 d	4 a
2 e	5 b
3 f	6 c

• Direct students' attention to the definitions. Students match the compounds with their definitions without using a dictionary.

• Students then check their answers using a dictionary. Feedback.

Answers
1 pen-friend
2 tourist attraction
3 night life
4 rock concert
5 package holiday
6 hotel room

2

• Students complete the sentences with an appropriate compound noun from exercise 1.

Answers
1 package holiday
2 tourist attraction
3 night life
4 rock concert

Optional activities

• Provide more noun pairs for students to match to make compound nouns. Write each half on separate pieces of paper and give one to each student.

• Students mingle to find a matching noun.

• Alternatively, students work in groups and lay the pieces of paper face down on a table.

• Students take turns to turn over two words and see if they match. If they do, the student keeps the match. If not, the words are turned face down again.

Listening (page 19)

Warm up: write these words on the board:
spaghetti, bouzouki music, tequila

• Ask students which countries the words are associated with (Italy, Greece, Mexico).

• Write the three countries on the board. In groups students brainstorm other things associated with each country. Feedback.

1

• Explain to students that they are going to listen to three people talking about Italy, Greece and Mexico.

• Students work in pairs and discuss what people can see and do in Italy, Greece and Mexico in more detail. Feedback and add students' ideas to the three items on the board.

For example:

Italy: *eat pizza, see the Coliseum, take a ride in a gondola*

Greece: *eat moussaka, visit the islands, ride on a donkey, see the Parthenon*

Mexico: *visit the pyramids, see a volcano, see Aztec monuments, eat tortilla, wear a sombrero, go swimming, see traditional native art.*

• Students listen to the tape to find out if the three people mention anything they have discussed. Feedback.

Answers

Italy: pizza, Coliseum
Greece: islands, ouzo
Mexico: Aztecs, pyramids, volcanoes

2 🔊

• Students skim read the true/false statements. In pairs, they try to remember whether the statements are true or false.

• Explain to students that they are going to listen a second time, but this time they need to listen more carefully for specific information to check their guesses.

• Play the tape again. Feedback, encouraging students to give reasons for their answers with reference to what they heard (see tapescript).

Answers

Speaker 1
  1 true (three kids)
  2 false (...haven't had an English breakfast for ages)
  3 true (He wasn't very impressed with the Coliseum)
Speaker 2
  4 false (There was no boat that day. So we went to Santorini)
  5 false (we actually visited the volcano)
  6 true (we've been touring for three weeks)
Speaker 3
  7 false (it isn't the first time I've been to Latin America)
  8 true (it's about 3,000 metres above sea level)

Tapescript (exercises 1 and 2)

SPEAKER 1

I can't stand the way a lot of British tourists go to other countries for their holidays and expect to find everything exactly as it is back home. I remember my brother turning up on our doorstep here in Rome with his wife and three kids, (question 2, 1) the whole family, and he expected a typical English breakfast. I mean, I've been living here for nearly ten years now and I haven't had an English breakfast for ages (question 2, 2). He also said he preferred English pizza to Italian pizza! The thing is, local people have their own customs which I think we've got to respect. When we went sight-seeing, my brother wasn't very impressed with the Coliseum, (question 2, 3) either, and it must be one of the world's top tourist sites.

SPEAKER 2

Oh yes, it's been a great holiday. We've spent most of it going from island to island – I think we must have visited half a dozen. We set off wanting to go to this tiny island called Folegandros but there was no boat that day. So we went to Santorini, (question 2, 4) and spent an evening there before we caught the boat the next day. I've never seen such a beautiful island before, and we actually visited the volcano, too. (question 2, 5) Very mysterious and romantic. Anyway, from there we went on to Folegandros,

which was very quiet and peaceful – unlike Santorini, which is really lively with lots of night life. Then we ended up here in Milos – you know, back to the cosmopolitan lifestyle again! We've had a good time, and drunk lots of ouzo, but it's great to be going home again – we've been touring for three weeks now. (question 2, 6) It's nice here, but I feel more relaxed at home than anywhere else, I think.

SPEAKER 3

I've just got back from Mexico. I was there on a business trip. I spent most of the time in Mexico City, which is absolutely huge. It must have a population of about 20 million by now. I've been to lots of places – it isn't the first time I've been to Latin America, (question 2,7) actually – but I've never seen anything quite like this before. As the plane was coming in to land, you could see this huge city, going on forever. It's about 3,000 metres above sea level, I believe, (question 2, 8). The Aztecs chose it as their capital and you can see the Aztec pyramids just outside the city, about one and a half hour's drive away. You can also see a volcano smoking away in the distance.

Grammar 2   (page 19)

Present perfect continuous

Presentation: introduce the concept of the present perfect continuous by asking these questions:
What's the date today?
When did we start English lessons?
Elicit: *We've been having lessons for two months/since October.*
I've been teaching this class for two months/since October.

• Write these two examples on the board. Elicit from students the meaning/use of the present perfect continuous.

Grammar box

• Direct students to the example in the grammar box on page 19. Ask students these concept questions:
Am I still waiting? (Yes)
How long have I been waiting? (two hours)

• Focus on the form of the present perfect continuous. Write *live, learn* on the board. Students work in pairs and make examples with the present perfect continuous and the verbs. Tell them to use the grammar box for help.

• Ask concept questions like the ones above to check students understand how to use the present perfect continuous.

Am I still living here?
How long have I been living here?
Are you still learning English?
How long have you been having English lessons?

I

- Students match the sentences in list A with the sentences in list B.

- Feedback, encouraging students to explain why each tense is used.

2

☆ Text notes

- Ibiza is one of the Spanish Balearic Islands in the Western Mediterranean. It is very popular with young British tourists who are attracted to the night life during the summer.

- Introduce the exercise by asking if any of the students have been to Ibiza and why they think it is popular.

- Explain that in preparation for the exercise, students are going to check the meaning of some words. Ask students these check questions:

What do invaders do? (They go to another country, like an army to conquer it)
Are invaders welcome by the people who live there? (No)
If someone is retired what have they done? (They have stopped work, usually because of old age)
What is a club? (Somewhere people go to at night to enjoy themselves)
What is a clubber? (Someone who likes going to clubs a lot)

- Students complete the text with the correct form of the verbs. Feedback, encouraging students to give reasons for their answers.

Answers

1 has been (and it still is)
2 have gone (so far, up to the moment of writing)
3 have seen (from a point in the past up to the present)
4 we've been coming here (we are still coming here; focus on how they've been coming)
5 has changed (completed action; we see the results)
6 has got/has been getting (action may or may not be complete; continuing process)
7 has become (completed action, results are visible in the present)
8 threw (definite complete event at a specific point in time)
9 have died (action may or may not be complete: ie more people could die)

Vocabulary 2 (page 20)

Travel

I

- Students complete the sentences using the words given. Feedback.

Answers

1	reserve	5	booking
2	board	6	miss
3	cancel	7	return
4	packed		

- Check understanding by asking the following check questions:

When you reserve a seat, can someone else sit in it? (No)
Do you get on or off a ship when you board it? (get on)
If you cancel something, can you do it at a later date? (No)
Do you fill or empty a suitcase when you pack? (fill)
Are you early or late when you miss something? (late)
Do you go one way or there and back on a return ticket? (there and back)

2

- Write the four headings on the board. In groups, students brainstorm travel words to go under each heading. Feedback.

- Students work individually or in pairs to add the words in the box to the four lists. Feedback.

Answers

by air: flight, pilot, check in, turbulence, cabin crew
by train: coach, underground, guard, carriage, platform
by sea: deck, port
by bus: stop, motorway

- Students choose three of the words from the box and write definitions for them. Feedback.

Writing (pages 20–21)

Transactional letter (complaint to a language school)

Warm up: Ask if anybody has been to England or attended a summer course in England. Ask if there were any problems.

- Explain to students that they and a friend have won a free week in England.

I

- Students read the letter on page 20. Ask the following check questions:

Where in England are they going? (London)
How will they travel? (fly)
Who will show them London? (a guide)
What will they do in London? (have English lessons)
Do they need to take money with them? (No)
How will they get to London from Heathrow? (picked up)
Where will they stay? (in a hotel)
Where will they eat? (in the hotel)

• Explain that the trip was not successful. Students read the letter again and look at the notes written on it. Elicit from students what went wrong.

2

• Direct students to the letter on page 21.

• Elicit from students what tenses the letter is written in and why.

• Students work in pairs and underline the examples of the wrong use of the present perfect simple. Feedback by asking students to read each mistake and then correct it using the past simple. Encourage students to give reasons for their answers.

Answers

where we have spent – where we spent
we have had great difficulty – we had great difficulty
has charged – charged
we have received – we received
we have had – we had
In all cases the writer is describing a completed action at a definite time in the past.

3

• Elicit from students what style the letter is written in, formal or informal. Ask them to tell you which expressions/words make it a formal letter.

• Students work individually to put the expressions in the box under the correct heading. Feedback by asking students for their answers and asking whether each phrase is formal or informal.

Answers

Hi! – opening – informal
Best wishes – closing – informal
Lots of love – closing – informal
Dear Mr/Mrs/Miss/Ms Jones – opening – formal
Yours faithfully – closing – formal
Love and kisses – closing – informal
My dear Tom – opening – informal
Dear Mum and Dad – opening – informal
Yours sincerely – closing – formal
Dear Sir/Madam – opening – formal
Bye! – closing – informal

4

• Direct students' attention to the advert for Queen's School of English on page 21.

• In pairs, students read the advert. Ask these check questions to make sure they understand:

Which exam are you prepared for? (Cambridge)
Can you play sport there? (Yes)
Are the classes large? (No)
Do you have to cook or buy food? (No)

• Students read the advert again and the notes written on it. Elicit from students what went wrong.

• Explain that students are going to write a letter to complain to the school. Students work in pairs and answer the questions. Feedback.

Answers

1 formal
2a Dear Director   d I am writing this letter to complain.
 b Yours faithfully   e Moreover
 c Unfortunately   f Finally, I must add

5

• Assign the letter for homework. Remind students to use the plan on page 21, formal language and to include the points noted on the advert. Remind them to use the model letter in exercise 2 as a guide.

• In the next lesson students exchange and read the letters making any necessary corrections or changes.

• Mark the letters. Set a time limit in another lesson to give feedback.

Sample letter (170 words)

Dear Director,

My name is ... . I have just got back to Greece and I am writing this letter to complain about the summer course for teenagers I have just attended at the Queen's School of English. Unfortunately, I was very unhappy with a lot of things.

Firstly, the course was for Cambridge Exam preparation but my class was very mixed. I have been learning English for five years but some of the students in the class were beginners. Also, the classes were very large and I hardly spoke to my individual tutor.

Secondly, the sports facilities were not very exciting, just a dart board and table tennis. Moreover, the social events in the evenings were not included in the price and we had to pay extra for some of them. They were expensive.

Finally, I must add that the food tasted awful. We had the same every day.

I am sorry to make so many complaints, but I was very unhappy with the course and the facilities.
Yours faithfully,

Revision (Units 1–3)

Answers

1

1	becoming	7	prefer
2	find	8	are
3	have	9	asked
4	offer	10	has
5	have	11	taking
6	go		

2

1	C	4	A
2	B	5	A
3	D	6	A

3

1 I've never been to Paris before.
2 I haven't finished doing the washing up yet.
3 I have been living here for ten years.
4 I have already read this book.
5 They built this school ten years ago.
6 While we were watching the film, the lights went out.

4

1 came/was snowing
2 goes/forgot
3 think/is becoming
4 haven't seen/want
5 met/go
6 have been learning/make

5

1	untidy	4	modest
2	shy	5	boring
3	tight	6	formal

6

1	to	4	is
2	did	5	going
3	it	6	been

7

1	intelligent	6	curious
2	strong	7	interested
3	friendly	8	successful
4	sensitive	9	impolite
5	interesting	10	attractive

Song

I Can See Clearly Now

1

• Introduce the topic of the song by asking students to discuss these questions briefly with a partner. Feedback.

2 🔖

• Play the tape for students to listen to the song.

• Students listen to the song again and complete the lyrics. Feedback.

Answers

1 has gone
2 clouds
3 has gone
4 have disappeared
5 sunshiny
6 blue

I Can See Clearly Now

I can see clearly now the rain has gone
I can see all obstacles in my way
Gone are the dark clouds that had me blind
It's gonna be a bright, bright, bright, bright sunshiny day
It's gonna be a bright, bright, bright, bright sunshiny day

I think I can make it now the pain has gone
All of the bad feelings have disappeared
Here is the rainbow I've been prayin' for
It's gonna be a bright, bright, bright, bright sunshiny day

Look all around, there's nothin' but blue skies
Look straight ahead, nothin' but blue skies

I can see clearly now the rain has gone
I can see all obstacles in my way
Gone are the dark clouds that had me blind
It's gonna be a bright, bright, bright, bright sunshiny day
It's gonna be a bright, bright, bright, bright sunshiny day
It's gonna be a bright, bright, bright, bright sunshiny day
It's gonna be a bright, bright, bright, bright sunshiny day...

4 A touch of magic

Topics
Magic crop circles, the magician David Copperfield, shows

Grammar
Past perfect simple, past perfect continuous, *used to* and *would*

Vocabulary
Noun suffixes, adjective suffixes

Reading
'Magic circles': gapped text

Listening
Interview with a magician: multiple choice

Speaking
Describing photos (magic)

Writing
Narrative composition (short story describing a show)

Reading (pages 24–25)

☆ Text notes

• Crop circles (also referred to as corn circles) are patterns that began appearing in fields in Britain and other European countries in the 1980s. For a long time, nobody could explain how they had been made and some people believed they were the work of extra-terrestrial beings or alien visitors to earth. The reading text describes one more logical explanation for these circles.

• *Nature* is a serious academic scientific journal where interesting scientific discoveries are often published for the first time.

• UFO or Unidentified Flying Object refers to mysterious space vehicles perhaps from other planets.

1

• Use the photographs on page 24 to establish the topic of the text. Students work in groups and discuss what they see. Feedback, encouraging them to guess what the photographs show.

2

• Explain that students are going to read a text which will tell them what they can see in the photographs.

• This is a scanning exercise. Students will need to look for specific information in the text, to answer the questions.

• Set a time limit (no more than 10 minutes). Advise students to scan the text and make a note of the numbers of the line(s) where the answers are given.

• Students compare answers in pairs. Feedback with reference to the text.

Answers

1 Someone who investigates crop circles (line 11)
2 A newspaper reporter (lines 19–20)
3 One of the two men who made crop circles (lines 23–27)
4 Large circular pattern which has been turning up mysteriously in English cornfields (lines 1–8)
5 A serious scientific magazine (line 45)
6 An unidentified flying object (not explained in the text but referred to in line 54, see text note)

3

• Direct students' attention to the gaps in the text. Explain that some information is missing.

• Students read through sentences A–E. Ask the following check questions:

What is another name for a flying saucer? (UFO)
Have many crop circles appeared in Britain and other countries? (Yes)
Does everyone believe they are created by visitors from outer space? (No)

• Explain that students will need to look at the words just before and just after each gap to understand the context before they decide which sentence belongs there.

• Students read the text carefully and decide which sentence belongs in each gap. Feedback, encouraging students to give reasons for their choices.

Answers

1	C	4	E
2	D	5	A
3	B		

4

• Students read the text again and in pairs put the events a–e in the order in which they happened. Remind students to include the missing sentences in exercise 3 when they are reading. Feedback.

Answers

1	b	4	a
2	e	5	d
3	c		

5

• Students read the text again and find phrases which have a similar meaning to the expressions. Feedback with reference to the text.

Answers

1 have been turning up (line 2)
2 had been taken in (line 32)
3 was spotted (line 57)

6

• Use this question to initiate a class discussion.

• Encourage brief responses to this question; if students have interesting things to say you may let the discussion develop more fully.

Grammar 1 (page 25)

Past perfect simple

Presentation: ask students how many ways of talking about the past they know. Elicit past simple, past continuous, present perfect, present perfect continuous.

• Students work in pairs and make example sentences for each tense.

• Write on the board: *When Helen got to the station yesterday, the bus had left.*

• Check students understand by asking these concept questions:

What did Helen do yesterday? (She went to the station.)
Did she catch the bus? (No.)

Why did she miss the bus? (Because when she got to the station, the bus had left.)

• Explain that *had* + past participle is called the past perfect. Elicit from students when the past perfect simple is used. Point out that it is a useful tense to use when telling stories or narrating something in the past.

Grammar box

• Direct students to the grammar box on page 25. Students read the example sentence. Check they understand by asking this concept question:

Which event happened first?

1

• Students read the text again to find and underline other examples of the past perfect simple. Feedback.

Answers

After he had talked to a newspaper reporter (line 18)
Delgado had been taken in (line 32)
had gone out of fashion (line 39)
what had caused the circles (line 43)
they had decided to make the first crop circle (line 48)
as if a UFO had landed (line 54)
had read newspaper reports (gap 5)
had heard about Australian farmers (gap 5)

2

• Students work in pairs and quickly read through the sentences deciding which event happened first. Feedback.

• Students work in pairs to make new sentences.

Answers

1 She didn't have any money because she had lost her purse.
2 He couldn't play football because he had broken his leg.
3 We left the theatre before the play had finished.
4 He didn't want to go to France although he had studied French at school.
5 I decided to ride my bike but someone had stolen it.

3

☆ Text notes

• David Copperfield is a famous American magician. His real name is David Kotkin and he has become famous for performing spectacular tricks, such as making ships and aeroplanes disappear.

• Establish the topic of the text by asking if students have ever seen a magician perform. Elicit the kinds of tricks he or she did.

• Students complete the text with the past simple or past perfect simple using the words in brackets.

Answers

1	had not yet changed	6	made/had made
2	had not yet learned	7	started
3	changed	8	learnt
4	had written	9	had been
5	saw	10	had already become

Vocabulary 1 (page 26)

Noun suffixes

Warm up: in groups, students brainstorm job titles. Feedback.

1

• Write *teacher, doctor, musician, journalist* on the board. Ask students to identify the suffixes (*-er, -or, -ian, -ist*).

• Point out that the suffixes are often added to nouns or verbs to make nouns to describe people's jobs.

• Students make nouns from the words given to describe people's jobs.

Answers
1	politician	6	performer
2	reporter	7	artist
3	journalist	8	sailor
4	producer	9	pianist
5	competitor	10	magician

Optional activity

• Give the students more examples of the above job nouns with suffixes and ask them to do the reverse, ie make the nouns into words without the suffixes.

scientist, printer, publisher, singer, engineer, writer, electrician

2

• Students skim through the text to get the gist and then complete it using the appropriate form of the word given. Feedback.

Answers
1	performers	7	suspicious
2	magician	8	choose
3	journalists	9	computer
4	prove	10	scientific
5	writer	11	scientist
6	carefully		

• Use the question to initiate a brief class decision.

Listening (page 26)

☆ Text note

• This interview has been adapted from a real interview. The tricks described actually occurred.

1 ▱

• Explain to students that they are going to hear an interview with a magician who went to see a performance by David Copperfield.

• Students look at the pictures and in pairs discuss the tricks that David Copperfield might have performed. Feedback.

Answers
1 The magician separated the top half of his body from the bottom.
2 The magician made the Statue of Liberty disappear.
3 The magician floated in mid-air in a cube.
4 The magician flew over the audience.

• Students listen to the tape and number the tricks in the order they hear them. Feedback.

Answers
a	3	c	2
b	1	d	4

2 ▱

• Explain that students are going to listen to the tape a second time but this time they will need to listen more carefully for specific information.

• Students read the statements and in pairs decide which key words they should listen for.

• Students listen again and choose the correct answer.

• Students compare answers in pairs. Feedback.

Answers
1	A	4	B
2	B	5	C
3	B		

Tapescript (exercises 1 and 2)

INTERVIEWER: Lorenzo Manzani, you're a magician yourself. Are you influenced by other magicians?

LORENZO: Yes, of course. We all are. Last week, for instance, I went to see the magician David Copperfield perform. I'd never seen him live before. It won't be the same seeing him on TV from now on. I was able to learn a lot about magic from watching him. I had a seat in the seventh row, so I saw everything that happened on stage. (question 2, 1)

INTERVIEWER: How long have you admired Copperfield?

LORENZO: I haven't always been a fan of David Copperfield. You see, in the past, I was jealous of his ability to capture the attention of the audience. I thought he was a show-off. (question 2, 2) He got all the girls. Well, all that has changed. I've changed ... David's become the standard for all magicians to aim for. Whenever I tell people I'm a magician they say, 'How did that Copperfield guy make the Statue of Liberty disappear?' My response is always to say the man is brilliant.

INTERVIEWER: Can you describe the show for us a bit?

LORENZO: David started his show with the Elevator. If you've seen him do this on TV, great; if not, I'll try and describe it for you ...

The curtain opens, and there's a cage, looking like an elevator, about six metres above the stage. Then they raise the thin screens on the front and back of the cage and you can see that that the cage is absolutely empty because you can see completely through it. Then they lower the screens again. Slowly the lights go down and it gets darker. Then, from the empty space above the cage, the shadow of a man begins to drop until the complete silhouette of David Copperfield can be seen behind the screen in the cage. He stands there in the cage as it descends. When it stops on the stage, David steps out. Now you're on your way with him into his dreams and nightmares, which is what the show's called. (question 2, 3)

INTERVIEWER: Did you learn anything new from the show – as a magician?

LORENZO: Well, one of the new acts I hadn't seen before was the Laser, which I must say was interesting. First of all, it looks as if someone is shooting a laser at David's belly, burning through his waist. After this, his upper body begins to rotate – to go round and round. (question 2, 4) Then his upper body seems to move onto a platform while his legs remain where they were. In the end, David puts his whole body together again and walks off the stage. This act is really cool.

INTERVIEWER: Amazing! Incredible!

LORENZO: The same goes for the Flying Trick. Which of us wouldn't love to fly with the birds! Humans have been trying to fly since the beginning of time and here's David flying around the stage, (question 2, 5) doing what we'd all love to do. The whole evening was like a story. David has captured our hearts with this show and his showmanship. I did notice a few things that went wrong in the production but I don't think anyone else noticed. David's a real professional.

Optional activity

• Initiate a class discussion by asking if students can explain how any of Copperfield's tricks are done.

Grammar 2 (page 27)

Past perfect continuous

Presentation: write these sentences from the text on page 24 on the board:

Bower told Delgado that they had been going around southern England creating new circles each year.
The artists had been deceiving fans of crop circles for a long time.

• Ask students to change the sentences using the past perfect simple:

The artists had gone around southern England creating new circles each year.

Bower told Delgado they had deceived fans of crop circles for a long time.

• Elicit from students the difference in meaning between the two forms. Point out that the sentences in the past perfect continuous emphasize the fact that the action was still continuing at some point in the past and the duration of the action. The past perfect simple suggests that the action was finished.

Grammar box

• Direct students to the first grammar box. Make sure they understand by asking the following concept question:

When did you start waiting? (half an hour ago)
Which event happened first? (the waiting)

1

• Students complete the sentences using the correct form of the verbs given. Feedback.

Answers
1 took
2 had arrived
3 had never seen
4 thought
5 had been waiting

Used to and would

Presentation: write these sentences on the board:

When I was at school, I got up at seven thirty every day.
The circus always came to town at Christmas time.

• Ask students to think of another way of talking about routine activities in the past. Elicit *used to*.

• Students reform the sentences using *used to*.

When I was at school, I used to get up at seven thirty every day.
The circus always used to come to town at Christmas time.

• Make sure students understand by asking these concept questions:

Do I still go to school? (No)
Do I still get up at seven thirty? (No)

• Explain that *used to* tells us that something often happened in the past but it doesn't any more.

• Point out that *would* is used in a similar way.

When I was at school, I would always get up at seven thirty.
The circus would always come to town at Christmas time.

Grammar box

• Direct students to the examples in the second grammar box. Students make example sentences using *used to* and *would*. Feedback.

2

• Students skim through the text to get the gist.

• Students complete the text individually or in pairs. Point out that more than one form of the past is possible especially when the choice is between the past simple, *used to* or *would*. Feedback, encouraging students to give reasons for their answers.

Answers
1 enjoyed
2 would keep/kept coming
3 would say/used to say
4 had seen
5 signed/used to sign/would sign
6 had been trying
7 had become
8 went/used to go
9 would always be/always used to be/was always
10 had never seen

Speaking (page 27)

I

• Explain to the class that they are going to describe two magic tricks and try and explain how they are done.

• Direct students' attention to the photos. Students describe briefly what they can see. Feedback.

Answers
1 a rabbit being produced out of a hat
2 a piece of rope being pulled through the magician's ear and out of his mouth

• Direct students to the expressions in the box. Students work in pairs to try and explain how these tricks are done using the expressions in the box to help them. Point out that they do not have to know the secret to the magic tricks but they can guess.

Vocabulary 2 (page 28)

Adjective suffixes

Warm up: elicit some examples of adjective suffixes by asking the following questions:

How would you feel in the following situations?
You made a silly mistake and everybody was looking at you. (Elicit *foolish*)
You win the lottery. (Elicit *lucky*)
Your parents offer to take you on a trip to your favourite country. (Elicit *enthusiastic*)

• Write the adjectives on the board. Students work in pairs to make nouns from the elicited adjectives. (*fool, luck, enthusiasm*)

I

• Students change the nouns into adjectives by adding the appropriate suffix. Point out that some adjectives do not need a suffix but that the spelling may still need to change. Feedback.

Answers
1 foolish   5 creative
2 funny   6 magical
3 enthusiastic   7 jealous
4 mysterious   8 brilliant

2

• Elicit some *-ed* and *-ing* adjectives by asking these questions:

If a lesson is about something you like, how will you feel? (interested)
How would you describe the lesson? (interesting)
If a concert you went to was cancelled, how would you feel? (disappointed)
If you thought the band was good but they performed badly, how would you describe the concert? (disappointing)

• Students complete the sentences with the correct form of an adjective from the list. Point out that some adjectives can be used more than once. Feedback.

Answers
1 surprised/astonished   5 excited
2 disappointing   6 boring
3 astonishing   7 astonished/excited
4 disappointed   8 depressing

Optional activity

• Students discuss what makes them disappointed, depressed, excited, astonished, surprised, bored.

Writing (pages 28–29)

Narrative composition

I

• Direct students to the photos. In pairs students describe what they can see. Feedback. Use the questions to initiate a brief class discussion.

Answers
1 trapeze artists in a circus
2 a fire eater performing outside on a sunny day

2

• Direct students to the words in the box. Check students understand them

• Students match the words with the pictures. Point out that some go with both pictures. Feedback.

Answers

applause – 1, 2	audience – 1, 2
street theatre – 2	in the open air – 2
act – 1, 2	trapeze – 1
perform – 1, 2	circus – 1, 2
acrobats – 1	fire eater – 2
costume – 1, 2	

3

• Direct students to the title of the text and ask them to predict what it is about (It describes a visit to a magician).

• Write these gist questions on the board:

What was the weather like? (freezing cold)
How long did they wait for the magician to appear? (15 minutes)
What was the last trick the magician performed? (He cut a woman in half.)
What did the audience do at the end? (they clapped)

• Students read the text quickly to find the answers. Feedback.

• Students read the text again to find and cross out ten extra words which should not be there. Feedback.

Answers

1 have (line 1)	6 has (line 12)
2 to (line 3)	7 did (line 15)
3 had (line 5)	8 and (line 16)
4 been (line 7)	9 been (line 20)
5 not (line 8)	10 the (line 21)

4

• Students find examples of each item in the composition. Feedback.

Answers

1 excited, magical, great
2 was/came/appeared/started/swallowed/did/cut/clapped
3 had never been/had booked/ had managed/had been
4 had been looking forward to/had been snowing/had been waiting
5 used to take us/would take us
6 At last/First of all/Then/The last

5

• Write these gist questions on the board. Students read the text quickly to find the answers. Feedback.

What kind of show does the text describe? (comedy)
What kind of student was he at school? (bad)
What was the last thing he did? (He sang a song.)

• Students complete the text with the sequencing words. Feedback.

Answers

Note: *Then* could go in various places in the text, apart from in first and last position.
1 As soon as
2 First of all
3 After that
4 Then
5 Finally

6

• Explain that students are going to write about an unforgettable show. They can write about a show they have seen or make one up.

• Direct students to the plan and give them time to answer the questions. Point out that these notes will make their composition interesting and cohesive.

• Assign the narrative for homework. Point out that it must end with the sentence: *It had been an unforgettable evening.* Remind students to use their notes, the plan and the vocabulary in this unit. Tell them to use the model composition in exercise 3 as a guide.

• In the next lesson students exchange and read compositions making any necessary changes or corrections.

• Mark the compositions. Set a time limit in another lesson to give feedback.

Sample composition (155 words)

When I was 12 I went to my first rock concert with my parents. We went to see _____ . My mum had bought the tickets in advance, so I had been waiting for two months when the day arrived. I was very excited.

The concert was in Athens, so we had to travel by train to get there. As we arrived in Athens we saw all the fans and the atmosphere was magical. Everyone was singing the band's hits, all the songs I had been listening to for two years.

First of all we found our seats and then waited for the concert to start. As soon as the music started everyone cheered enthusiastically and started to applaud. The band were brilliant. They played their recent hit and after that they played some of their old songs.

Finally they asked the audience to sing with them which was great fun. It had been an unforgettable evening.

5 Them and us

Topics
Boys and girls, relationships, neighbours and friends

Grammar
Comparatives and superlatives: adjectives and adverbs

Vocabulary
Feelings, relationships

Reading
'Boys will be boys': multiple matching

Listening
Talking about falling in love: blank filling

Speaking
Pairwork interview (favourite things)

Writing
Opinion article (friendship)

Reading (pages 30–31)

Warm up: Establish the topic of the texts by asking students to work in groups and brainstorm the personality differences between boys and girls. Feedback quickly.

1

• Explain that students are going to read and talk about the relationships between boys and girls.

• Make sure students understand the vocabulary by asking these check questions:

If someone goes on about something, do they talk a lot or a little? (a lot.)
When do you need a friend to be supportive? (When you have a problem.)
What does a supportive friend do? (They share your problem.)
If someone irritates you, how do you feel? (annoyed, angry)
Is it nice to be criticised? (No)
If you get on with someone, do you like them? (Yes)

• Students match the words and phrases in list A with the definitions in list B.

• This is a skimming exercise. Students will need to skim the text for specific words. Set a time limit. Students find and underline the words in the text.

Answers

1 e (Nicola, line 16)	4 d (Debbie, line 30)
2 f (Nicola, line 18)	5 b (Debbie, line 35)
3 c (George, line 19)	6 a (Lewis, line 42)

2

• This is a scanning exercise. Students will need to look for specific information in each text. They do not need to worry at this stage about any other details or difficult vocabulary.

• Students read the texts again and match the information with the correct student, A, B, C or D. Feedback encouraging students to make reference to specific points in the text.

Answers

1 D (There's nothing that you can talk about with them. That's really boring.)
2 C (What I don't like about boys is the way they change as soon as there are boys around.)
3 B (... they're more confident than girls)
4 A (Boys also boast a lot ...)
5 A (girls are more mature than boys)
6 C (They don't treat you as an equal any more.)
7 D (Most of my best friends are boys.)

Grammar 1 (page 31)

Comparatives and superlatives: adjectives

Presentation: write the following gapped sentences from the texts on the board and ask students to complete them using the correct form of the words in brackets.

People say it's because girls are _____ than boys. (mature)
It really is one of the _____things about them. (irritate)
Most of my _____ friends are boys. (good)

- Students check their answers with the texts. Elicit from the students which forms we use when we compare two things (comparative), more than two things (superlative).

Grammar box

- Direct students to the examples in the grammar box. Check students understand by asking why we say *taller* but *more confident* and *tallest* but *most mature*? (Because *tall* is a short adjective, one syllable; *confident* is a long adjective, with three syllables.)

- Students work in pairs and brainstorm more one syllable and two syllable adjectives. Feedback.

- Write *good, better, best* on the board. Elicit from the students that *good* is an irregular adjective. Students think of another irregular adjective like *good* (bad, worse, worst).

1

- Students read the texts again to find and underline examples of comparative adjectives. Students check their answers in pairs. Feedback.

2

- Students rewrite the sentences using the adjective given. Feedback.

Answers
1. Bill is younger than Susan.
2. Maggie is shorter than Peter.
3. Bob is a more dangerous driver than Jane.
4. Susan is more successful than Bill.
5. Susan is the most intelligent student in the class.
6. I am better at physics than at maths.

3

★ **Text notes**

- Ricky Martin is a pop star from Puerto Rico. One of his most famous songs is 'Living the Vida Loca' (Crazy Life). Puerto Rico belongs to the United States and Spanish and English are both official languages.

- Cricket is an English sport played with a bat and ball and two teams of 11 players. Cricket games have a reputation for lasting a long time and being very slow.

- Ask students what they know about Ricky Martin. Students read the text quickly to find out where he's from, what he was like at school and which subject he disliked.

- Students read the text again and complete it with the correct form of the adjectives. Point out that sometimes, more than one adjective is possible but that students must think carefully about the context. Feedback.

Answers
1. most famous/important/beautiful/interesting/best
2. most beautiful
3. best
4. fresher
5. favourite
6. the most useful
7. worst
8. most irritating
9. most disgusting
10. most boring
11. most useful/important

Listening (page 32)

★ **Text notes**

- Romeo and Juliet are the lovers in Shakespeare's tragedy *Romeo and Juliet*, written in about 1600.

- Arnold Schwarzenegger (1947–) is an Austrian actor. He has very rugged looks and is most well known for his role in the film *Terminator*.

- Leonardo DiCaprio (1974–) is an American actor, popular with young female fans and well known for his role in the film *Titanic*.

1

- Explain that students are going to listen to a talk about love and that in preparation for the listening they are going to check the meaning of some words.

- Students match the words in list A with their definitions in list B. Feedback.

Answers
1 b	4 c
2 d	5 e
3 a	

2

- Students listen and renumber the items in exercise 1, list A in the order in which they hear them on the tape. Feedback.

Answers
1 masculine	4 head over heels in love
2 blush	5 fade
3 stage	

3

- Students work in pairs and try to complete the notes from memory.

- Students listen again and check their answers. Feedback by asking students to give the whole sentence, not just the missing word or phrase.

Tapescript (exercises 2 and 3)

PSYCHOLOGIST

Human beings are more interested in love than in anything else. Most pop songs are about love. But what exactly happens when people fall in love? Well, scientists have been studying the phenomenon of love and it seems that love is a less romantic business than we thought.

Take a man who walks into a room. Let's call him Romeo. The first stage of falling in love is when he sees a woman. We'll call her Juliet. Why does Romeo find Juliet more attractive than all the other women in the room? First of all, he likes the size and shape **(question 3, 1)** of her face. Juliet also likes the size and shape of Romeo's face; she likes his straight figure and the fact that his face isn't too masculine. Research has shown that women are more likely to be attracted to the soft features of Leo DiCaprio than the square face of someone like Schwarzenegger.

As Romeo gets closer, his heart beats faster. **(question 3, 2)** He blushes slightly, he sweats a little and his hair begins to shine more brightly. This is because his head produces a kind of oil that makes his hair look brighter. He is already in the first stages of love.

For love to develop, both the man and the woman must have similar feelings. Romeo thinks that Juliet is the most important person in the world and she feels the same way about him.

The next day, Romeo has reached the second stage of falling in love: his brain **(question 3, 3)** releases a substance called dopamine every time he thinks of Juliet, and this makes him feel good. But he doesn't know that what he's feeling is the effect of the dopamine; he thinks he's falling in love. He feels more and more attracted to Juliet. She is continually in his thoughts and he can't get her out of his mind **(question 3, 4)** – not that he really wants to, because even the thought of her makes him feel good.

One Saturday, Romeo and Juliet go out shopping and they reach the third stage of falling in love. By now they are head over heels in love with each other. They are so crazy about each other that they become blind to each other's faults. **(question 3, 5)** No one in the world is more perfect than their partner.

Then they enter the fourth stage of love – the make or break stage. If their bodies are not still producing the right chemicals, their love may fade. What might keep them together are substances called endorphins. Endorphins calm the mind and reduce anxiety, though the feelings they produce are not as powerful as the feelings Romeo and Juliet experienced when they first started to go out together. But now they feel warm and safe. **(question 3, 6)** They have become dependent on each other – they say they can't live without each other. **(question 3, 7)** It's true love at last.

Vocabulary 1 (page 32)

Feelings

1

• Students read through the sentences in list A and underline the adjectives in each one.

• If they are unsure of the meaning, refer them to the reading text on pages 30 and 31.

• Students match the beginnings of the sentences in list A with their endings in list B. Feedback.

Answers

1	g	5	e
2	c	6	d
3	b	7	a
4	f		

2

• Students read the definitions and write an adjective which fits each one. Point out that students can find the adjectives in exercise 1.

Answers

1	proud	4	jealous
2	afraid	5	upset
3	embarrassed		

Optional activity

• Initiate a brief class discussion about when students have felt proud, embarrassed, afraid, upset or jealous.

Speaking (page 33)

Warm up: in groups, students discuss what films they have seen at the cinema recently. What did they think of them? Encourage them to give opinions and to decide which film was the best. Feedback quickly.

1

• Students look at the sentences and underline the superlative in each one.

• Students work individually and complete each sentence. Do not feedback at this stage.

2

• Direct students to the question words in the box.

• Students use the question words to form questions from the sentences in exercise 1. Feedback.

• Explain that students are going to use these questions to interview a partner about their answers to exercise 1. Direct them to the examples and point out that they should follow up their question with other questions to find out more information.

• In pairs, students interview each other. Feedback.

Early finishers

• Early finishers can interview another student who has also finished.

• Alternatively early finishers can write down the answers they got from their partners.

Grammar 2 (page 33)

Comparatives and superlatives: adverbs

Presentation: demonstrate some common adverbs by performing the following actions, eliciting from the students how you are doing each action: walk quickly, walk slowly, cough loudly, speak quietly.

• Write the elicited adverbs on the board.

Grammar box

• Direct students to the grammar box on page 33.

• Make sure students understand by asking these questions:

Who speaks more quickly, your mum or your dad?
Which moves more slowly, a tortoise or a snake? (tortoise)
Which student in class speaks the loudest?
When do we use comparative adverbs? (to compare two actions.)
When do we use superlative adverbs? (to compare three or more actions.)

• Point out that many comparative and superlative adverbs have the same form as the comparative and superlative adjectives. Elicit some examples from students and write them on the board:

fast/faster/fastest
easy/easier/easiest
hard/harder/hardest
early/earlier/earliest
late/later/latest

I

• Students complete the three sentences from the listening text with an appropriate adverb formed from the adjectives given. Students check their answers in pairs. Feedback.

Answers

1 His heart beats faster.
2 His hair begins to shine more brightly.
3 He blushes slightly.

2

• Students complete the sentences using an appropriate comparative adverb formed from the adjectives given. Feedback.

Answers

1 more seriously	5 more carefully
2 harder	6 more loudly
3 better	7 farther/further
4 more fluently	

Optional activity

• Students interview each other using the completed questions.

3

• Establish the topic of the text by asking students to read the title and predict what the text is going to be about. Feedback and ask if any of them know what the planets Mars and Venus represent. (Mars – war, Venus – peace).

• Students skim the text to check their predictions.

• Students read the text again and choose the correct form. Students check their answers in pairs. Feedback.

Answers

1 more dangerously	7 faster
2 fewer	8 more slowly
3 more safely	9 less
4 better	10 better
5 more quickly	11 more carefully
6 even more surprising	

Vocabulary 2 (page 34)

Relationships

I

• Students skim through the expressions in the box. Make sure they understand them by asking what the expressions have in common (refer to relationships).

• Explain that there are two groups of expressions, positive ones about becoming friends (Coming together) and negative ones about stopping friendships (Breaking up). Students put the expressions under the correct heading as a class.

• Point out that most of the expressions are followed by prepositions.

Answers

Coming together: get on (with)/make friends (with)/be close (to)/be crazy about/fancy/fall in love (with)/go out (with)/have a date (with)/arrange to meet
Breaking up: fall out (with)/break up (with)/have a row (with)/go off /get divorced (from)/separate (from)

2

• Students work in pairs to complete the sentences using words and phrases from exercise 1. Feedback.

Answers

1 crazy about   4 fancies
2 row   5 date
3 love

3

• Write *friend* on the board and elicit from students words and phrases which derive from this word. Explain that they can make compound nouns, adjectives or adverbs, nouns and verbs.

• Make a list or draw a mind map using students' ideas. Here are some words to include in your diagram.

friend: *friendly, unfriendly, friendship, boyfriend/girlfriend, pen friend*

• Students complete the sentences with words made from *friend*. Feedback.

Answers

1 pen friend   4 friendship
2 unfriendly   5 friendliest
3 boyfriend

Writing (pages 34–35)

Opinion article

Warm up: in groups students brainstorm ways to express opinions in English. For example: *In my opinion, I think, I believe, in my view.*

• Explain that this section focuses on writing an opinion article for a magazine. Elicit from students what things they think are most important when writing opinion articles. For example:

You have to express your opinion clearly.
Give examples and reasons to back up your opinion.

Make it clear – use paragraphs.
Make it interesting – use clear, lively language and don't be afraid to be controversial.
Use neutral to formal language.
Use connectors, such as *first of all, also, finally*.

1

• Use the picture on page 34 to establish the topic of the article. Students discuss in groups what they can see in the picture. Feedback by asking students what they the article is going to be about (neighbours).

• Direct students' attention to the adjectives in the box. Make sure they understand them.

• Students discuss the questions with a partner using expressions from the box for question 3. Feedback with the whole class.

Suggested answers

1 friendly, helpful, quiet
2 A good neighbour says hello/asks about you and your family/tells you if someone called while you were out/lends you something if you need it/invites you to their parties/reports to the police if they see something suspicious
   A good neighbour does not make a lot of noise/ignore you when they see you/refuse to help you/invite you to parties/make a mess and not tidy up/gossip about you
3 Students' own ideas.

2

• Students read the connectors in lists A and B. Make sure they understand them by asking these check questions:

Which connectors could you use at the beginning of an article? (firstly, first of all)
Which could you use at the end? (in conclusion, to sum up)
Which could you use to add to an opinion? (in addition, as well)
Which could you use in a conclusion? (in conclusion, therefore, to sum up)
Which could you use to give a personal opinion? (in my opinion, in my view)

• Students match the connectors in list A with those in list B.

Answers

1 c   4 b
2 f   5 a
3 e   6 d

3

• Students read the title and predict what the text is going to say about neighbours. Feedback.

• Point out that a catchy title will get the reader's interest, which is the aim of an opinion article.

• Students skim the text to check their predictions were correct.

• Students read the text again. Do not ask them to complete it at this stage. They should read it to understand the sequence of the article.

• Students read again and complete the text. Point out that there is more than one possibility for each gap. Feedback.

Suggested answers

1 Nowadays/Today/In my opinion
2 First of all/Firstly
3 in addition
4 In my opinion/In my view
5 for example
6 Finally/To sum up

4

• Students work in pairs and put the labels next to the appropriate paragraph. Feedback asking students to identify which phrase or sentence helped them to make a decision.

Answers

Paragraph 1: introduces the topic
Paragraphs 2 and 3: develop the topic
Paragraph 4: reaches a conclusion

5

• Students read the text again and complete the advice to focus on other aspects of the language and style. Feedback in pairs.

Answers

1 respects, helps, are rare, do not ask, do not make
2 should
3 first of all, nowadays, in conclusion
4 to get reader's interest
5 stating an opinion at the beginning and giving a strong conclusion.

6

• Explain that students are going to write a similar opinion article to the one on neighbours. The title is *What makes a good friend?* Direct students' attention to the words and expressions in the box. Make sure they understand them.

• Students work in pairs and discuss the questions using words from the box for question 3. Point out that they should keep notes on their answers. They will need these notes later.

7

• Direct students' attention to the plan. Students answer the questions using their notes from exercise 6.

• Assign the article as homework. Remind students to use the plan, their notes, the vocabulary in this unit and a catchy title. Tell them to use the article in exercise 3 as a guide.

• In the next lesson students exchange and read articles making any necessary changes or corrections.

• Mark the articles. Set a time limit in another lesson to give feedback.

Sample article (156 words)

Fantastic friends!

A good friend has a lot of good qualities. I think the most important is loyalty. A good friend never lets you down. My best friend, Helen is loyal and she is always there when I need her.

In my view, a good friend will stand by you when you have problems. For example, if I have a row with someone, Helen will listen and try and be supportive. She will also give good advice and come up with a solution to a problem.

In addition, a good friend would not gossip about me. Helen has never said things about me behind my back and she would not listen to gossip about me. Nowadays, it is difficult to find friends like this.

In conclusion, the most important things in a good friend in my opinion are loyalty and support. You need someone to stick by you when you have problems and to help you find solutions.

6 Starstruck

Topics
Astronomy, the future

Grammar
Future simple and *going to*, present continuous and present simple (for future)

Vocabulary
Noun suffixes, collocations and phrasal verbs with *set*

Reading
'A star is born': multiple matching (headings)

Listening
Interview with an astronomer: true/false

Speaking
Discussion (future plans)

Writing
E-mail message (describing a school trip)

Reading (pages 36–37)

☆ Text notes

• VLT stands for very large telescope. One of the most famous in the world is the American Hubble telescope. The text describes another VLT which will enable astronomers to discover exciting new facts about the universe and even understand the origins of the earth. It may even enable us to travel back in time by seeing images from the distant past.

• The Andes is a mountain range in South America stretching from Chile through Argentina to Columbia.

• London buses are usually double-decker buses, that is passengers sit upstairs and downstairs.

• Eta Carinae is the name of a star which was discovered quite recently.

• Ultraviolet light is beyond the purple end of the range of colours that people can see.

Warm up: Establish the topic of the text by asking students to quickly name important space events, for example, landing on the moon.

1

• Ask students to quickly discuss what they think might be discovered in space in the future. Feedback briefly.

• This is a skimming exercise. Students look at the photo and read the text quickly to answer the questions. Advise students to make a note of the line number in which they find the information. Feedback with reference to the text.

Answers
1 It is a VLT – a Very Large Telescope (lines 1–2)
2 In the Chilean Andes. (line 5)
3 It is useful because it allows scientists to see things they have not been able to see before. (line 10)

2

• Students work in pairs to match the words in list A with the definitions in list B. Feedback but do not correct at this stage.

• Students read the text again (scan) to find and underline the words in list A. Advise them to make a note of the line numbers.

• Students work in pairs to check their answers. Point out that reading the word in context may help them with the definition. Feedback with reference to line numbers in the text to encourage students to think about vocabulary in context.

Answers
1 g (line 1)   5 b (line 34)
2 h (line 3)   6 c (line 12)
3 f (line 4)   7 e (line 19)
4 a (line 7)   8 d (line 25)

3

• This is a gist exercise. Students read to understand enough to complete the exercise. They should not worry about other details at this stage.

• Students work individually to match the headings with the correct paragraphs. Encourage them to underline any key words or ideas that help them find the correct answer. Feedback, encouraging students to give reasons for their answers.

Grammar 1 (page 37)

Future simple and *going to*

Presentation: elicit examples of the future simple and *going to* by asking these questions:

What are you going to do next?
What are you going to do tomorrow?
How old will you be on your next birthday?
What day will it be the day after next?

• Write the examples on the board.

• Elicit from the students how many ways they have just used to talk about the future (*going to* + infinitive, *will* + infinitive).

Grammar box

• Direct students to the grammar box on page 37. Students read the examples. Check they understand them. Ask students to find another use for *will* that you have not presented yet (for decisions made at the time of speaking).

1

• Students complete the sentences from the text and then check their answers with the text. Feedback.

Answers

1 will allow
2 is going to be
3 will reveal

• In pairs, students think about why these two different forms of the future are used. Give them prompts like the following to help them:

Which one do we use to make predictions about the future?
(both)
Which one do we use to express intention? (going to)
Which one do we use to make predictions based on evidence that we can see now? (going to)

2

• Students choose the correct future form for each sentence. Feedback, encouraging students to give reasons for their answers.

Answers

1 will (decision made at the moment of speaking)
2 going to (intentions, decisions already made before the moment of speaking)
3 going to (plans already made before the moment of speaking)
4 going to (decision made before the moment of speaking)
5 going to (prediction made on evidence that we can see now)
6 going to (plan already made)
7 will (prediction)
8 will (decision made at the moment of speaking)

3

• Write *Happy New Year* on the board. Elicit from students when new year is and what people usually do. Elicit *make resolutions*.

• Direct students to the examples. Focus on the use of *going to*.

• Direct students to the box of words and expressions. Check they understand them. Students write down their resolutions using the words and phrases. They show them to their partner and compare and discuss them. Feedback.

Speaking (page 38)

Warm up: introduce the topic by asking students to guess what they think you are going to do in the future. Use these questions as prompts:

Do you think I will be rich?
Do you think I will live in the city or the country?
Do you think I will have a large family?
Do you think I will play a musical instrument?
Do you think I will travel around the world?

1

• Direct students to the pictures on page 38. In pairs, students quickly say what they can see in each picture. Feedback.

• Explain that students are going to discuss their future plans using the pictures for ideas. Ask which form of the future they might use most and why (*going to* for plans and intentions). Point out the examples under the pictures.

• Students read the instructions and do the exercise. Feedback by asking students what their partner is and is not going to do.

Early finishers

• Students write a summary of the points made by their partner. Feedback.

Vocabulary 1 (page 38)

Noun suffixes

Warm up: write the following words from the reading text on the board and elicit what parts of speech they are (verb or noun).

explode (verb)
collision (noun)

• Ask students what the noun from *explode* is (explosion) and what the verb from *collision* is (collide).

• Explain to students that you are going to focus on nouns ending in *-tion, -sion* and *-ion*.

1

• Students match the verbs in list B with the definitions in list C. Feedback.

• Students then add *-tion, -sion,* or *-ion* to the verbs to make nouns for list A. Students check answers in pairs then feedback.

Answers
1 expansion, expand – get bigger
2 construction, construct – build
3 invention, invent – make something new
4 education, educate – teach
5 pollution, pollute – damage the environment
6 revision, revise – go over work again
7 permission, permit – allow
8 observation, observe – watch carefully
9 prediction, predict – guess the future
10 possession, possess – own

2

• This exercise consolidates the words from exercise 1. By this stage, students should be able to do this task quite quickly. Feedback, asking two students to read out the sentences. Student 1 should read the original sentence and student 2 the transformation.

Answers
1 revision	4 education
2 permission	5 suggestion
3 description	6 construction

Listening (page 39)

☆ Text notes

• This is an interview with a physicist/astronomer, Francisco Sanchez, who talks about some of the recent achievements of astronomy and what we can expect in the future.

• The Canary Islands, a group of islands in the Atlantic, near Africa, belonging to Spain: Tenerife, Las Palmas, Lanzarote, Fuertaventura, Gran Canaria, Palma, Gomera and Hierro.

• Big Bang, the idea that the universe began with a huge explosion. The theory says the pieces resulting from the explosion are still flying apart.

Warm up: use the photograph on page 39 to introduce the topic. Students discuss in pairs what they can see (the universe).

1

• Students discuss the questions in pairs. Do not expect correct answers. The aim is to introduce them to some of the topics that are discussed on the tape. Feedback, but do not confirm students' answers yet.

2 🎧

• Students read through the statements and possible answers and underline key words and ideas to help them focus their attention as they listen to the tape. For example: *discovered* (question 2), *the Big Bang take place* (question 3), *the biggest telescope* (question 4), *the universe* (question 6).

• Students can also try and predict the correct answers.

• Students listen to the tape and choose the correct answers. Feedback, asking students to make reference to specific things they heard on the tape (see tapescript).

Answers
1 B	5 C
2 C	6 A
3 C	7 B
4 A	

Tapescript (exercise 2)

SANCHEZ: ...This is an opportunity I'm not going to miss. When it is finished, this telescope will be one of the most powerful in the world. It means Spain will go into the twenty-first century as a leader in scientific progress ...

INTERVIEWER: Welcome to another Science In Action. That was Francisco <u>Sanchez, one of the world's greatest astronomers,</u> (question 1) who has told Science In Action that he hopes to be one of the first people to look through the enormous telescope that is being constructed in La Palma. The Institute of Astrophysics in the Canary Islands is one of the best in the world and Sanchez has made <u>discoveries that allow us to see what stars are like inside.</u> (question 2) He has discovered and explored black holes and has helped us understand the Big Bang which began the universe. We asked him how he felt when looking at the stars.

SANCHEZ: Looking at the stars makes me ask who I am. We can see so little with the naked eye, but now we have invented telescopes of such power that we will soon know more about where we come from and where we are going.

INTERVIEWER: Do we know for certain where we came from?

SANCHEZ: Yes, nowadays we know much more about how the universe began. We know it all started with a great explosion in a very small part of space. We also know that the Big Bang took place about 14,000 million years ago. (question 3)

Now, if we can build telescopes that reach galaxies at those distances, we'll be in a position to say how the universe was born. Telescopes are real time machines. With the new telescope that we're building at La Palma we will get very close to understanding how the universe began. Our telescope will be the biggest in Europe. (question 4)

INTERVIEWER: Do we know what's going to happen to humanity? What's the end of the world going to be like?

SANCHEZ: Well, from the point of view of astronomy, yes, in a few years' time we'll be able to see how the stars were born and how they die. This knowledge will help us to predict how the stars will develop, including the earth. We already know that our sun was formed 6,000 million years ago and that it will come to end in about 5,000 million years. (question 5) It will turn into a huge red-hot ball, its atmosphere will get bigger and bigger, and it will eventually swallow up the earth.

INTERVIEWER: What's going to happen in astronomy in the twenty-first century?

SANCHEZ: I believe we're going to learn a lot of new things – about ninety per cent of the universe is still unknown. (question 6) We're going to find out much more about distant galaxies, how the earth started and how beautiful things like a man or a woman were created.

INTERVIEWER: One final question. Have we ever been visited by extra-terrestrial beings? Do you think we will be one day?

SANCHEZ: You know, I'd love to look through my telescope one fine evening and come face to face with a visitor from outer space who will say, 'Hey, colleague, it's me!' Many people say they've seen aliens – but I think if someone does visit us one day they'll probably think we're crazy! (question 7) At any rate, I doubt very much whether aliens have ever visited us.

3

• Use the question to initiate a class discussion about the future. Encourage students to refer to ideas on the tape during the discussion.

Grammar 2 (page 39)

Present continuous and present simple (for future)

Presentation: introduce the concept of the future with present continuous and present simple by drawing two faces on the board. Call them Paul and Mary. Ask students to listen for and make a note of the way the speakers talk about the future as you read this dialogue between Paul and Mary.

Paul: Hey, I've got two tickets for the Pearl Jam concert on Saturday. Do you want to come?
Mary: I can't. I'm going to London.
Paul: Oh, that's nice. When are you leaving?
Mary: I'm leaving in the morning.
Paul: When are you coming back?
Mary: On Sunday.
Paul: Are you flying?
Mary: No, I am going by train.
Paul: Great! What time does your train leave?
Mary: It leaves at 7.30.
Paul: Oh, I'm free then – do you want me to give you a lift to the station?

• Elicit from the students the two forms of the future:

Present continuous: *I'm going to London/When are you leaving? I'm leaving in the morning/ When are you coming back? Are you flying?/I'm going by train.*

Present simple: *What time does your train leave? It leaves at 7.30.*

Grammar box

• Direct students to the examples in the grammar box. Elicit from them when these forms of the future are used (present continuous: for plans, programmes and arrangements; present simple: for fixed or scheduled events (often fixed by someone else, not the speaker).

1

• Students choose the correct tense in each sentence.

• Students check their answers in pairs. Feedback, encouraging students to give reasons for their choices.

Answers

1. is (fixed event)
2. starts (programme)
3. does the train for Glasgow leave (programme, timetable)
4. am having (plan)
5. are doing (plan)
6. am working (plan or arrangement)

2

• Students skim through the text to identify what kind of text it is (a horoscope). Ask these check questions to make sure students understand:

Are horoscopes pessimistic or optimistic? (optimistic)
What do horoscopes use to predict the future? (planets and stars)

• Students work individually and choose the correct future form in each case.

• Students check their answers in pairs. Feedback, encouraging students to give reasons for their answers.

Answers

1. are going to have (prediction based on evidence we see now)
2. are going (plan/arrangement)
3. will be (prediction)
4. will change (prediction)
5. will turn up (prediction)
6. go on (scheduled event)
7. is only going to ask (prediction based on evidence)

Vocabulary 2 (page 40)

Collocations and phrasal verbs with set

Warm up: Elicit from students any collocations or phrasal verbs with *set* they know.

• Encourage them to give examples of their use.

• Introduce the following collocations by miming simple actions: *set the table, set fire to something, set foot on, set a trap.*

• Ask students to look at the collocations with *set* on page 40 and to guess which ones you are miming.

• Use these questions to elicit more collocations with *set*:

If a hunter wants to catch an animal, what does he do? (He sets a trap.)
If a prisoner is found innocent, what will the court do? (Set him free.)
Parents do not want their children to smoke, so they set an example. What do they do? (They avoid smoking themselves.)

When the astronaut Armstrong set foot on the moon, what did he say? (One small step for man, one giant leap for mankind.)

1

• Students work individually and choose four of the collocations. They write an example sentence for each one. Feedback.

2

• Students work individually to complete the quiz with collocations and phrasal verbs with *set*. Students check answers in pairs. Feedback.

Answers

1	foot on	5	fire
2	record	6	table
3	off	7	free
4	off	8	up

3

• Treat this as a fun activity.

• Students do the quiz with a partner. Give students time to think about their answers and then start the quiz. Students answer alternative questions. Feedback by asking students to call out the answers.

Answers

1. Neil Armstrong
2. Green
3. 1492
4. 1961
5. because they want to build on the land
6. students give personal answer
7. Nelson Mandela
8. Switzerland

Writing (pages 40–41)

E-mail message

Warm up: establish the topic of the text by asking students who has e-mail and what they use it for.

1

• Students read the questions and discuss their ideas with a partner. Feedback.

2

• Students read the e-mail message on page 41. Elicit from them whether the language used is formal or informal. Encourage them to give examples. (E-mail messages tend to be informal and have many of the features of conversation between friends).

- Students read the email message again and answer the questions. Feedback.

Answers

1 Tony
2 Maria
3 Yes
4 Maria knows about Tony's exams and his holiday plans. Also the informal nature of the language, for example the vocabulary: great, glad, what about you; ellipsis (words left out): glad, can't wait. The opening: Hi and the closing: Write soon/Bye for now
5 Prague
6 No, he's going with the school

3

- Students read Maria's reply to Tony's e-mail and answer the questions. Students check their answers in pairs. Feedback.

Answers

1 To a Greek island, Rhodes or Corfu
2 To acknowledge receipt of Tony's message and to comment briefly on it
3 Paragraph 3 (I'm going to do lots of sunbathing/snorkeling/swimming/shopping/etc)
4 That's all for now/Keep in touch
5 Which teachers are going?

4

- Students read the list of features of informal speech. Elicit examples from students of each type.

- Students work in pairs to find and underline examples in Maria's message. Feedback.

Answers

1 it's, they'll, we'd, I'm, we'll, it'll, we're, that's
2 to put up with, make up our minds (= decide), sit around, keep in touch
3 great to hear from you
4 go: go somewhere/to go to/go shopping
    do: do a lot of swimming/do lots of sunbathing
    get: get there

5

- Elicit from students some examples of the future forms presented in this unit. Encourage students to tell you when each one is used.

- Students read both messages again and underline all the examples of future forms. Students work in pairs and discuss the meaning of each example. Students number them accordingly. Feedback, bearing in mind that the future is subjective and plans and intentions can be expressed by the same form at the same time.

Answers

Tony's message: you're planning (1), is going to (1), are you going (1), are you staying (1), are you planning (1), are you going (1), don't spoil (3) **Maria's message:** are voting (1), they'll have to (3), we leave (2), are planning (1), I'm going to do (1), we'll probably (3), it'll be quicker (3), we're meeting (1), I'll let you know (1).

6

- Explain that students are going to write their own reply to Tony's e-mail message. They decide where they are going to go for their holiday (they can make something up, for example the Bahamas, Mexico, the Greek islands, Paris in the Spring!).

7

- Direct students to the plan on page 41. Students work in pairs and make notes using the questions to help them. Point out that notes will help to make their message more cohesive. Feedback.

- Assign the message writing as homework. Remind students to use their notes, the paragraph plan, informal language and the vocabulary in this unit.

- In the next lesson students exchange and read messages making any necessary changes or corrections.

- Mark the messages. Set a time limit in another lesson to give feedback.

Sample message (174 words)

Dear Tony,

Hi, just got time to write a quick reply to your message. So, you're going to Prague – lucky thing. I'm sure you'll have a great time.

Great news! Mum and dad are taking us to Paris on Friday. We're staying for five days and my cousin Christina is coming too! I'm really looking forward to it. We're flying to Paris, which I've never done before.

We've already planned how we're going to spend the time. In the mornings, we're going to tour the city to see all those famous sights – but we're also going to Versailles. We'll probably go to Disneyland for a day too. In the afternoon, we're just going to stroll around, perhaps do a bit of shopping and sit at those lovely pavement cafes. One evening, we're definitely going to take a boat ride along the Seine – everyone says it's a real treat!

Well, that's all for now. I hope you have a nice time in Prague. I'll drop you a line from Paris.

Write soon.

Bye for now,

Revision (Units 4–6)

Answers

1

1	drove	5	will be/is
2	had already left	6	will be
3	'd never flown	7	had won
4	are you going to do		

2

1	fast/slowly or carefully	5	seriously
2	dangerously	6	carefully
3	fast/hard	7	easily/harder
4	dangerously		

3

1	set foot	5	set free
2	sets sail	6	set out
3	setting fire	7	set a new world record
4	set a trap	8	set the table

4

1 used to play
2 'm going to be
3 'm having a tooth
4 had never been to
5 had been snowing

5

1 ✓
2 of
3 he
4 ✓
5 ✓
6 ✓
7 been
8 them
9 about
10 ✓

6

1 B
2 D
3 A
4 B
5 D
6 B
7 D
8 B
9 C
10 D

Song

Lucky Star

• Direct the students to the photograph on page 43. Students discuss briefly what they know about Madonna.

1

• Direct students to the words in the box. Make sure they understand them. Students work in pairs and put the words into rhyming pairs. Feedback.

Answers

far–star
lost–cost
stay–may
side–guide
glow–know
bright–light

2 🔲

• Students listen to the song and tick the words from exercise 1 they hear. Feedback, also asking students which words are not in the song.

Answers

star, glow light, bright, know, guide, side, far, may
Not in song: lost, stay, dark, cost, park

3 🔲

• Students listen again and correct the sentences.

Answers

1 wherever you are
2 may be
3 you'll be my guide
4 all right
5 luckiest by far

Lucky Star

You must be my lucky star
'Cause you shine on me wherever you
    are
I just think of you and I start to glow
And I need your light
And, baby, you know

Starlight, star bright, first star I see
    tonight
Starlight, make everything all right
Starlight, star bright, first star I see
    tonight
Starlight, yeah

You must be my lucky star
'Cause you make the darkness seem so
    far
And when I'm lost you'll be my guide
I just turn around and you're by my
    side

Starlight, star bright, first star I see
    tonight
Starlight, make everything all right
Starlight, star bright, first star I see
    tonight
Starlight, yeah

Come on, shine your heavenly body
    tonight
'Cause I know you're gonna make
    everything all right
Come on, shine your heavenly body
    tonight
'Cause I know you're gonna make
    everything all right

You may be my lucky star
But I'm the luckiest by far

Starlight, star bright, first star I see
    tonight
Starlight, make everything all right
Starlight, star bright, first star I see
    tonight
Starlight, yeah

Come on, shine your heavenly body
    tonight
'Cause I know you're gonna make
    everything all right
Come on, shine your heavenly body
    tonight
'Cause I know you're gonna make
    everything all right

You may be my lucky star
What you do to me, baby, you know
I'm the luckiest by far

Starlight, star bright, first star I see
    tonight
Starlight, let's get this thing all right
Starlight, star bright, first star I see
    tonight
Starlight, yeah

Photocopiable

7 Terrors of the earth and sky

Topics
Earthquakes, pollution, volcanoes, environmental problems and solutions

Grammar
Modal verbs: possibility, probability, certainty
Modal verbs: obligation, necessity, advice, permission
Modal perfect

Vocabulary
Homonyms, environment

Reading
'Earthquake!': environmental problems and solutions, multiple choice

Listening
Four speakers talking about environmental issues: multiple matching

Speaking
Information gap (what to do during a fire)

Writing
Advice leaflet (protecting the environment)

Reading (pages 44–45)

☆ Text notes

• The text is a leaflet giving advice to schoolchildren about what to do in case of an earthquake. It is divided into what do at school, what to do at home and what to do in the street if an earthquake occurs.

• *Crust* has several meanings. The most common is the hard outer surface of bread. We also use it to refer to baked outside part of foods such as pies. The sense in which it is used in the text is the thin, hard, dry surface of the earth.

• *Fault* also has several meanings. Its most common meaning is in the expression 'It's your fault'. The meaning in the text is a large crack in the rocks that form the earth's surface. When the two sides of this crack move we feel the effects as an earthquake.

1

• Use the pictures on page 44 to establish the topic of the text. Ask students to look at the pictures and in pairs to describe what they see. Feedback briefly.

• In pairs, students discuss which of these things they should and should not do in an earthquake. Feedback, encouraging students to give reasons for their answers. Do not confirm students' answers at this stage.

• Students read the leaflet and tick the pictures which give the correct advice. Set a time limit. Students check their answers in pairs. Feedback with reference to the text.

Answers
Pictures 1, 5 give correct advice
'get under the desk immediately' (line 12)
'... try to find a large open space to wait in.' (line 43)

2

• Students read the true/false statements and in pairs decide if each one is true or false.

• Students read the leaflet again to check their answers. Feedback with reference to the text.

Answers
1 True (lines 4–5)
2 False (lines 11–13)
3 False (lines 29–34)
4 False (lines 37–40)
5 True (lines 43–44)
6 True

3

• Students find the words in list A in the text and underline them. Students then match the words with the correct definition in list B, using the context in the text.

Answers
1 c (line 8)   4 a (line 15)
2 e (line 2)   5 b (line 25)
3 d (line 3)

Grammar 1 (page 45)

Modal verbs

Presentation: elicit from students some modal verbs and write them on the board:

will, would, may, might, shall, should, can, could, must/have to, ought to

• Ask the following questions to find out how much students know about modal verbs:

What do they have in common? (they are followed by the infinitive, they form the interrogative by inversion)

When do we use modal verbs? (to express possibility/probability/certainty/necessity, etc)

Grammar box

• Direct students to the grammar box on page 45. Students read the examples.

1

• Students scan the text to find and underline the modal verbs. Feedback, asking students how many different modals they found.

Answers

may have (line 2), may cause (line 4), can travel (line 9), may be (line 10), should get (line 11), should at the same time go (line 13), must not argue (line 15), should walk (line 27), must wait (line 21), can find (line 34), must not go (line 34), can come out (line 36), must leave (line 37), should walk down (line 38), should not use (line 38), may be (line 38), could find (line 39), could also be (line 44) There are five different modal verbs (may, can, should, must, could).

• Students match the meanings of the modal verbs they have underlined to the examples given in the grammar box. Point out that some of the meanings will be dealt with in Grammar 2.

2

• Students choose the correct modal verb in each sentence. Remind them to refer back to the grammar box. Feedback, encouraging students to give reasons for their answers.

Answers

1	must (near certainty)	4	may (possibility)
2	might (possibility)	5	should (probability)
3	will (certainty)	6	might (possibility)

3

• Establish the topic of the text by asking students these questions:

Are there frequently/often forest fires in your country? Have there been any forest fires recently? What causes them?

• Elicit modal verbs from the students as they put forward their ideas about what causes the fires.

• Students complete the text with the modal expressions. Point out that there may be more than one possible answer for each space. Feedback.

Answers

1 will probably be/may be
2 could destroy
3 may be/will simply be/will probably be
4 can't be
5 can't be
6 must be
7 could reduce
8 may be

Listening (page 46)

☆ Text notes

• Ozone is a layer of gases that stops harmful radiation from the sun reaching the earth. One of the speakers explains that there are two kinds of ozone, one good, one bad. The good ozone protects earth from the sun's rays. Bad ozone comes from exhaust fumes and causes pollution.

• Ozone depletion is the reduction of the ozone layer caused by using harmful substances found in fridges, sprays and car fumes.

• *Boycott* means to stop doing something for example buying a certain product as a form of protest.

• *Haze* is a kind of light mist or fog.

Warm up: use the pictures on page 46 to introduce the topic of the environment and pollution. In groups, students look at the pictures and brainstorm what they know about pollution and its causes. Feedback briefly.

1

• Explain that in preparation for the listening exercise, students are going to check the meaning of some words.

• Students match the words in list A with their definitions in list B. Feedback.

Answers

1	d	3	b
2	c	4	a

2

• Students work in pairs and use the pictures and the words in exercise 1 to predict what the text is going to be about.

• Students listen and check their predictions. Feedback, focusing on the points which connect the pictures with the vocabulary.

3

- Students skim through the statements and underline the key words which provide specific information.

- In pairs, students try to remember which speaker mentioned each piece of information.

- Students listen to the tape again to check their answers. Feedback asking students to refer to specific things they heard on the tape (see tapescript).

Answers

A Speaker 2 (I think we can all help and we must do our bit)
B Speaker 3 (use sunscreen lotion and apply often every two hours)
C Speaker 2 (we should all boycott products)
D Speaker 4 (there is in fact both good and bad ozone)
E Speaker 1 (I can't be bothered to wear a cap)
F Speaker 3 (don't be fooled by clouds)

Tapescript (exercises 2 and 3)

SPEAKER 1

We had a lesson at school about the ... er ... I can't remember what you call it now – oh yes, it was about the ozone layer. It's the damage done to the ozone layer – and the teacher said we've got to do something about it because the hole's getting bigger and bigger every year. The hole over the arctic or the antarctic – I can't remember which – is now bigger than Europe, I think she said. She was telling us yesterday that we have to be careful in the summer when we go to the beach or play basketball. We should wear a cap and long sleeves, but <u>I can't be bothered to wear a cap</u> **(question E)** – it gets in the way and falls off. I do wear a T-shirt because it can get very hot, but that's all.

SPEAKER 2

Yes, I do think it's a serious problem. Cases of skin cancer have certainly increased, which is very worrying. If we're going to stop the damage to the ozone layer, we should cut down on the use of things like aerosols. <u>I think we can all help and we must do our bit</u>. **(question A)** I've stopped using aerosol sprays myself and I think <u>we should all stop using products</u> **(question C)** with chemicals that damage the ozone layer. Unfortunately, there aren't any fridges that use environmentally-friendly chemicals, but even not opening your fridge too often helps. If we don't do these things, they say that by 2010 the hole in the ozone layer will be as big as a country like Canada.

SPEAKER 3

It's easy to protect yourself against the harmful effects of the sun's rays. Here are a few simple suggestions. First of all, you should never stay in the sun for long periods of time without protection. You should wear at least a sunhat, a T-shirt and shorts, and you should use sun cream. <u>Sun cream should be put on every two hours when you're outside.</u> **(question B)** You should pay special attention to the parts of your body that are most exposed to the sun: your ears, face, neck, shoulders, back, knees and the top of your feet. Wear sunglasses and <u>don't be fooled by clouds</u> **(question F)** – the sun's rays can penetrate light clouds.

SPEAKER 4

Many people don't realize that not all ozone is the same. <u>There is in fact both good and bad ozone</u>. **(question D)** The good ozone surrounds our earth, from fifteen to thirty-five kilometres above its surface. It's like a filter, preventing most of the sun's dangerous rays from reaching the earth. Without this layer, many more people would get skin cancer and eye diseases. Plants and the surface of our oceans would also be damaged. Bad ozone, on the other hand, is found at ground level and it comes from sources such as car exhaust. In the summer months, you can see the grey smog it causes over cities where the air doesn't move very much.

Optional activity

- Students jot down two or three things that they can do to fight pollution and protect themselves from its effects, using what they have heard on the tape.

Vocabulary 1 (page 46)

Homonyms

Warm up: tell students these English jokes and explain how they depend on words which have the same spelling and pronunciation but have different meanings:

How do you know when an elephant is going on holiday? It packs its trunk. ('trunk' = an elephant's nose/a large box-like suitcase)
Which driver never has accidents? A screwdriver (driver = a person who drives a car; screwdriver = a kind of tool)

1

- Students match the words in the box with the definitions. Feedback.

Answers

1	roots	5	bark
2	leaves	6	rock
3	branch	7	ground
4	trunk		

• Students look at the words in the box again and in groups brainstorm how many meanings they can think of for them. Feedback.

2

• Students complete the sentences using words from exercise 1. Feedback, checking the meaning of each word. Use the notes in brackets.

Answers
1 rocked (mime this movement from side to side, pretending to be holding a baby)
2 ground (mime the action of grinding coffee beans)
3 branches (ask how many branches of a certain local bank they can name)
4 barking (make a barking sound)
5 trunk (hold your arm up to your nose and mimic an elephant)

Speaking (page 46)

I

• Use the picture on page 46 to establish the topic of the exercise.

• Students work in pairs. Student A looks at the information on page 104, student B looks at the information on page 113.

• As students hear the advice, they should keep notes. Feedback, making sure students use modal verbs followed by infinitives as they give the advice.

Answers
Student A: keep calm, do not use the lifts, follow your teacher's instructions, make sure all the windows are closed, call the fire brigade, don't panic
Student B: shut all doors, keep fire doors closed

Early finishers

• Students who finish early write down the five most important things to do when there is a fire in the building.

Grammar 2 (page 47)

Modal verbs

Presentation: elicit from students what advice they would give to a friend who is going to go sunbathing. Encourage them to use the modals they heard in the listening exercise.

• Elicit from students which modal verbs are used to give advice (should, must).

Grammar box

• Direct students to the grammar box on page 47 and point out the use of the modal verbs to express obligation, necessity, advice and permission. Check their understanding by asking them to identify specific examples in the grammar box.

Give me an example of a modal verb used to give permission. (may, can't)
Give me an example of a modal verb used to give advice (should, ought to)

• Students add one more example to each category.

I

• Students read (skim) the text to answer this gist question. *What kind of eruption is most likely to happen?* (long, calm eruption, 90 per cent chance)

• Students read the text again and choose the correct modal verb in each case. Feedback, encouraging students to give reasons for their answers.

Answers

1	could	7	can
2	could	8	will
3	might	9	will
4	might	10	should
5	could	11	should
6	must		

2

• Students complete the second sentence so that it has a similar meaning to the first sentence. Feedback.

Answers
1 We needn't use plastic bags to carry the shopping.
2 Everyone has to pay the fees before lessons begin.
3 The travel agent said I/we had to be at the airport two hours early.
4 Do we have to have the air conditioning on?

Modal perfect

Grammar box

• Direct students to the modal perfect grammar box on page 47.

• Ask students to change these sentences into the past:
It may rain tomorrow. (yesterday) (It may/might have rained yesterday.)
She must be on holiday. (She must have been/gone on holiday.)

• Write on the board:
Modal + have + past participle

• Explain that when we are not sure about something in the past we use this pattern. Write this question and answer on the board:
How big was the earthquake?
I don't know. It must have been six on the Richter scale.

• Make sure students understand by asking these concept questions:
When did the earthquake take place? (In the past.)
Do we know how big it was? (No, we're not sure.)

3

• Students choose the correct modal verb in each case. Feedback, encouraging students to give reasons for their answers.

Answers
1	must	4	must
2	can't	5	can't
3	may		

Vocabulary 2 (page 48)

Environment

Warm up: students brainstorm in groups some of the examples of pollution mentioned in the listening exercise. Feedback.

1

• Explain that the words listed in A and B can be combined to make phrases which can be used to talk about environmental problems.

• Students match the words in list A with the words in list B. Students check their answers in pairs. Feedback.

Answers
1	b	5	d
2	a	6	g
3	f	7	e
4	c		

Optional activity

• Check understanding of the above concepts by describing a problem and asking students to guess which one you are describing:

throwing waste away in places where we shouldn't (dumping rubbish)
a layer of gas which protects us from the rays of the sun (ozone layer)
animals which are threatened with extinction (endangered species)
pollution caused by the gases cars produce (exhaust fumes)
hotter weather than we used to have (global warming)

2

• Students work in pairs to think of any solutions to the problems in exercise 1. Feedback briefly.

• Explain that the words listed in A and B can be combined to make phrases which can be used to talk about solutions to environmental problems.

• Students match the words in list A with the words in list B to find some possible solutions to the problems in exercise 1. Students check their answers in pairs. Feedback.

Answers
1	e	4	f
2	a	5	b
3	d	6	c

3

• Students read the comments and match them with the problems and solutions from exercises 1 and 2. Direct them to the example first. Feedback.

Answers
1 exhaust fumes/leave the car at home
2 ozone layer/ban aerosols
3 dumping rubbish/recycle rubbish
4 endangered species/protect animals

Writing (pages 48–49)

Advice leaflet

☆ Text notes

• Genetic engineering can be used to grow crops and breed animals which cannot be harmed by diseases. Some people are afraid that scientists may produce clones using this technique.

• Genetically Modified Food is food which has been produced with the help of science. It may help to solve the problem of hunger and provide cheap food but some people say it has less nutritional value and causes diseases like cancer.

1

• Introduce the topic of the exercise by asking students to read the title of the leaflet and predicting what it is going to be about.

• Students skim the text to check their predictions.

• Direct students to the words given. Make sure they understand them.

• Students complete the text using the words. Feedback, asking students to tell you which word or phrase in the text helped them to make their choices.

Answers

1	water	6	destroying
2	forests	7	pollute
3	food	8	global
4	genetic	9	environment
5	polluting	10	recycling

2

• Point out that each paragraph in the leaflet needs a heading. Direct students to the list of possible headings. Explain that they do not need all of them.

• Students work in pairs to label each paragraph. Feedback, with reference to the text.

Answers

Paragraph 1 C	Paragraph 3 A
Paragraph 2 B	Paragraph 4 E

3

• Explain to students that they are going to read the leaflet in detail and that answering the questions will help them to focus on the format.

• Students read the leaflet more carefully and answer the questions in pairs.

Answers

1. Paragraph 1 – 3 points
   Paragraph 2 – 3 points
   Paragraph 3 – 4 points
   Paragraph 4 – 2 points
2. should, might
3. Students express their own opinions.
4. Students express their own opinions.

4

• Explain that students are going to write their own leaflet to advise people on what they can do to help protect the environment.

• Students work in pairs and put the pictures under the correct heading. Feedback

Answers

at home: a, g, h
in the shops: d, e
in the street: b, c, f, i

• Students work in pairs and describe in detail the environmental problem associated with each picture and the solution for each problem. Encourage them to use the grammar and vocabulary in this unit.

• Feedback, encouraging students to first state the problem, then a solution using modal verbs.

5

• Assign the leaflet as homework. Remind students to use the headings given and the grammar and vocabulary in this unit.

• In the next lesson students exchange and read leaflets making any necessary changes or corrections.

• Mark the leaflets. Make time in another lesson for feedback.

Sample leaflet (164 words)

What you can do to protect the environment - take action now!

At home
Don't waste water! Having a bath may be fun, but it wastes water! You should take a shower and save water!
Stop dumping rubbish. You should recycle your rubbish.
Protect the ozone layer. You should not use aerosol sprays because of the fumes.

Shopping
People waste a lot of plastic bags when they go shopping and plastic products cause a lot of pollution. You should remember to take a basket with you or you can use a bag made out of other material - not plastic!

In the street
Pollution from exhaust fumes does a lot of damage to the ozone layer. It is one of the causes of global warming. You should not use your car for short distances - you can walk or use your bike instead.
Conclusion
We can do a lot to save our planet when we are at home, shopping and in the street.
We must act now!

The happiest days?

Topics
Schooldays, successful learners, the importance of play, school improvements, a perfect day

Grammar
First and second conditionals, zero conditional

Vocabulary
Common verbs, collocations with common verbs, phrasal verbs with *go* and *get*

Reading
'Why playing is important for kids': gapped text

Listening
Discussion about school breaks and holidays: true/false

Speaking
Pairwork task (planning a school curriculum)

Writing
Descriptive article (a perfect day)

Reading (pages 50–51)

☆ Text notes

• There is a saying in English, 'Schooldays are the happiest days of your life'.

• Hide and Seek is a traditional children's game where one child has to find the others, who are hiding.

• Hopscotch is a traditional children's game. It involves throwing a stone onto numbered squares drawn on the pavement with chalk and then hopping from square to square. The game is often played in the school playground.

• *Recess* is an American word for *break*.

Warm up: introduce the topic of the unit by asking students to read the title and predict what it is going to be about. Feedback briefly.

• In pairs, students quickly discuss what they consider to be their happiest days so far. Feedback. Ask students whether they think schooldays might be the happiest days.

1

• Students read the statements and decide whether they agree or disagree with them. Students discuss their opinions in pairs. Feedback, eliciting these points:

pupils work too hard/do not work hard enough
most pupils are more interested in having fun than studying
happy pupils are better pupils, so games are good for learning
children with lots of friends who play a lot also do well in life

2

• Establish the topic of the text by asking students to read the title and predict what it is going to be about. Feedback quickly.

• Students read the text to find out whether the writer agrees or disagrees with the statements in exercise 1. Set a time limit. Advise students to underline the part of the text where they find the answer. Feedback, with reference to the text.

Answers
1 Agrees (line 26), (lines 50–52)
2 Disagrees (line 28), (line 44)
3 Agrees (line 29), (line 44)
4 Agrees (line 35)

3

• Point out numbers 1–6 in the text. Explain that these numbers mark the position of missing sentences.

• Students read sentences A–F carefully and underline words which will help them to put the sentences into the correct place in the text.

• Students read each paragraph carefully, focusing on the space where a sentence is missing. Point out that they should read what comes before and after the space and make connections with the missing sentences. Feedback with the whole class, eliciting which words and phrases helped them decide where the sentences go.

Answers

1 B (... to move their legs ... they play traditional games)
2 C (... if local government plans go ahead)
3 E (paragraph goes on to give the contrary opinion to the previous paragraph)
4 D (... tend to be more successful at school)
5 F (... if a child spends more time with friend ... you learn to take turns and cooperate)
6 A (... finding it more difficult to get on with children of the same age)

4

• Students read the definitions. In pairs, students try to guess the words. Students check their guesses by reading the text again, including the missing sentences. Feedback with reference to the text and sentences.

Answers

1 chase (B)
2 traditional (line 9)
3 centuries (line 12)
4 evidence (line 26)
5 research (line 31)

Grammar 1 (page 51)

First and second conditionals

Grammar box

Direct students to the grammar box on page 51 and ask students to read the example sentences. Make sure they understand by asking these concept questions:

Do people usually visit Rome? (yes)
Do they usually see the Coliseum? (yes)
Are you likely to win first prize? (no)

• Elicit that the first conditional is used for future events which are likely to happen and the second conditional for future events which are unlikely to happen.

1

• Students read the text to find and underline sentences with *if*. Feedback with reference to the text.

Answers

'If you ask school children ...' (line 1)
'If local government plans go ahead ...' (line 13)
'children would learn more if they didn't waste so much ...' (line 19)
'children would learn to read and write better if ...' (line 23)
'if youngsters played more ...' (line 28)
'if children spend more time with ...' (line 30)
'if a child spends more time with friends ...' (line 40)
'if you play well, you ...' (line 42)

• In pairs, students divide the sentences into first and second conditionals. Remind them to use the grammar box to help them.

2

• Students work in pairs to expand the notes to make first and second conditional sentences. Explain that in some cases the form they choose will depend on what they think they are going to do in life. Feedback, encouraging students to explain why they have chosen each form. Point out the use of contractions (*I'll, I'd*) and the fact that the two clauses can come in either order.

Answers

1 If I pass my exams, I'll go to University. (likely)
2 If I won the lottery, I'd buy a Porsche. (unlikely)
3 If I get a very good job, I'll throw a party. (likely) If I got a very good job, I'd throw a party. (less likely)
4 If I went to India, I'd hear many different languages. (unlikely) If I go to India, I'll hear many different languages. (likely)
5 If I'm free next Saturday I'll see my friends. (likely)
6 If I spoke Japanese, I'd go and work in Japan. (unlikely)
7 If I sit the First Certificate exam, I'll pass it. (likely)/If I sat the First Certificate exam, I'd pass it. (less likely)

3

• Students read the text quickly to find and correct the spelling errors. Feedback.

Answers

N - E - R - S - E (nurse)
P - H - O - T - O - G - R - A - F - E - R (photographer)

4

• Students complete the text using the verbs given. Remind them that they should read the whole text first to get the general meaning. This will help them to be more accurate when completing it. Feedback.

Answers

1 answer
2 will give
3 get
4 would do
5 will
6 were
7 would take
8 would fix
9 would take
10 stop

• Point out the use of *If I were... If I was ...* Explain that using *were* is more formal.

Listening (page 52)

Warm up: direct students to the question about holidays. Students briefly discuss it.

1

• Explain that students are going to listen to a radio discussion on school holidays and breaks.

• Students work in pairs and discuss the statements. Feedback, encouraging students to give reasons for their answers.

2 📼

• Explain to students that the speakers on the tape are the presenter, a schoolboy, and two schoolgirls. Students predict which people they think say each sentence from exercise 1.

• Students listen to the tape and check their predictions.

Answers

A	2	C	4
B	3	D	1

3 📼

• Students read the true/false statements. They try to guess the answer before listening to the tape a second time.

• Students listen for a second time and check their guesses. They should try and make a note of what each speaker says (see tapescript). Feedback.

Answers

Speaker 1
  1 False 2 True
Speaker 2
  3 True 4 True
Speaker 3
  5 False 6 True
Speaker 4
  7 False 8 False

Tapescript (exercises 2 and 3)

INTERVIEWER: How important are breaks at school? Should they be long or short? Should school holidays be shorter? Is the school day too long? To talk about these and other questions of interest to all schoolchildren, I have with me four students from a number of different countries. Let me start with you, Adrian Chapman. What do you have to say on the question of breaks?

SPEAKER 1: Well, we start school at nine o'clock (question 3, 1) every day and we have quite a long lunch break at one o'clock. We start again at two o'clock and then finish school at four o'clock. That's quite a long day, but I like the long break in the middle. The problem is that if we get a lot of homework we don't have much time to do it in. I mean, if you get home at around half past four, by the time you've had something to eat and watched telly a

bit you don't have much time for your homework. Perhaps it might be better if we started school a bit earlier and finished earlier. (question 3, 2) If we did, it would leave us time to relax for a while after school and do our homework as well.

INTERVIEWER: Thank you, Adrian Chapman. Now it's the turn of Margaret Montessori.

SPEAKER 2: I'm a bit worried about the summer holidays. I read in the paper that the government is planning to make the summer break shorter. They say children don't need such a long summer holiday. Well, I totally disagree! (question 3, 3) People who say things like that can't remember what it was like to be a child. If the government goes ahead with these plans, it'll make children less creative and more depressed than ever. Actually, the summer holiday is the only time in the year when we can escape from all those tests! We need to spend less time at school, not more. If we didn't have the long summer holidays, we'd never get the chance to play and discover the world in our own way. (question 3, 4)

INTERVIEWER: Strong words from Margaret Montessori. And now, Helen Spirou. Helen, what is your school day like?

SPEAKER 3: Well, in my school, we begin very early. It's a long and tiring day. It's a private school. The bus picks us up at about half past seven and the first lesson starts at eight o'clock. We have lots of short breaks between lessons, about fifteen minutes, and we have one which is a bit longer for about twenty minutes. (question 3, 5) That's when we have something to eat – just a snack. We don't really have time to eat much more. It's quite a hard day but the advantage is it finishes early. Two o'clock. And I'm usually home by three. That leaves me enough time to get my homework done. (question 3, 6) It's not bad, but if the breaks were longer we wouldn't feel so exhausted every day.

INTERVIEWER: Thank you, Helen. Now our final speaker, Mario Sabato.

SPEAKER 4: Well, our day is quite short, like Helen's. We finish at about one o'clock but we also have lessons on Saturday, which is horrible. I can't stand going to school on a Saturday morning. The weekends are for relaxing and doing things you enjoy. Of course, it's nice finishing early (question 3, 8) during the week but the weekend is a disaster. It would be better if we could have the whole weekend off like other schools in other countries. Besides, no one's in the mood for lessons on Saturday morning, not even the teachers, so we waste a lot of time. (question 3, 7) I'd be much happier – I think everyone would – if we were free on Saturdays.

Optional activity

• Initiate a class discussion using the following question: *Which speaker do you agree with most?*

Speaking (page 52)

• Students work in pairs to identify what they can see in the pictures. Feedback by asking these questions:

What school subjects can you see? (computers, geography, English)
What are the students doing? (taking an exam)
What about the timetable? How many breaks are there?

• Explain that students are going to discuss what changes they would make in their school, using the topics in the pictures and the verbal prompts given.

• Elicit from the students which conditional they are going to use most (second, as it is unlikely that they will ever have an opportunity to change things).

• Before students begin talking in pairs, brainstorm a few ideas and put them on the board. Remind students to use second conditionals where appropriate.

• Students work in pairs and choose three things to change. Feedback.

Early finishers

• Ask early finishers either to write down their proposals or come up with more than three changes.

• As students feedback, tell the rest of the class to listen and take notes. Ask other members of the class to say whether they agree or disagree with what the other pairs are suggesting.

Vocabulary 1 (page 53)

Common verbs

Warm up: elicit examples of the most common verbs in English.

1

• Write the following verbs on the board and elicit example sentences from students:
think, say, have, go, get, take, want, imagine, discover

• Students work in pairs and decide which seven of these verbs they think are the most common verbs in English. Feedback.

Answer
> think, say, have, go, get, take, want

2

• Students read and complete the sentences using the most common verbs from exercise 1. Feedback.

Answers
> 1 take
> 2 got
> 3 had
> 4 say
> 5 think
> 6 have, get
> 7 want

Grammar 2 (page 53)

Zero conditional

Presentation: Write these example sentences on the board and ask students how they are different.

a *If the government goes ahead with these plans, it will make children less creative.*
b *If you play well, you learn well.*
c *If we get a lot of homework, we don't have much time to do it in.*
d *I'd be much happier if we were free on Saturdays.*

Answers
> a present simple + will
> b present simple + present simple
> c present simple + present simple
> d would + past simple

• Elicit which one is an example of the first conditional (a) and which one is an example of the second conditional (d).

• Explain that (b) and (c) are examples of the zero conditional. Elicit that the zero conditional is often used to express general rules, truths or cause and effect.

Grammar box

• Direct students to the grammar box on page 53 for more examples of the zero conditional. Point out the use of the imperative in the last example.

1

• Students match the beginnings of the sentences in list A with the endings in list B. Feedback.

Answers
> 1 f   5 b
> 2 e   6 a
> 3 g   7 d
> 4 c

2

• Establish the topic of the text by asking students if they listen to music while they are doing their homework. Elicit why, when and what type.

- Students read the text before completing it to find out what kind of music is mentioned in the text. (Classical)

- Students complete the text individually or in pairs. Feedback with the whole class.

Answers

1 have	6 is
2 feel	7 make
3 tend	8 increases
4 work	9 turns
5 do	

Vocabulary 2 (page 54)

Collocations with common verbs

Warm up: play a collocation game. Write each common verb (*have, get, go, make, do*) on separate pieces of paper. Write some of the collocations that go with these verbs on separate pieces of paper (*shopping, walking, a shower,* etc).

- As students come into class, give them a piece of paper. When each student has a piece of paper, ask someone in the class to read out what is written on their piece. Everybody listens and checks to see if their word matches the one they heard. For example, student 1 reads out *do*. Student 2 reads out *the shopping*. It is likely that more than one student will match each common verb. Continue until all the students have found a match.

1

- Students read the verbs in list A and the words and phrases in list B and match them to make collocations. Feedback. Ask students to write their answers in their vocabulary notebooks.

Answers

1 c	4 b
2 e	5 d
3 a	

2

- Students complete the sentences using the correct form of the verbs. Feedback.

Answers

1 did	4 got
2 have	5 make
3 been	6 have

Phrasal verbs with *go* and *get*

Warm up: elicit any phrasal verbs that students know with *go* and *get*. Encourage students to make example sentences.

3

- Students match the phrasal verbs in list A with their definitions in list B. Feedback, asking students to give example sentences.

Answers

1 d	4 c
2 e	5 a
3 f	6 b

4

- Students read the text quickly and then complete it using the phrasal verbs in exercise 3.

Answers

1 get away	4 had gone off
2 get by	5 get over
3 went back	

Writing (pages 54–55)

Descriptive article

1

- Students read through the text for gist to answer these questions:

Is this person spending his/her perfect day at home? (no)
How many countries does he/she go to? (four)

- Students read the text again and mark the points where *would* is missing.

- Direct them to the example in the text before they start. Feedback.

Answers

1 would have no homework
2 would really begin
3 would be shining
4 would have a free ticket
5 would also be with me
6 would go swimming
7 would have lunch
8 would sit in a café
9 would show me round
10 would come back
11 would end

2

• Students read the text again and divide it into four paragraphs. Students work in pairs. Feedback with reference to the text.

Answers

Introduction: from the beginning to '... no homework either'
Morning: from 'My perfect day would really begin...' to '...clear Caribbean Sea'
Afternoon: from 'Then we would have lunch ...' to 'his latest film'
Evening: from 'In the evening'... to 'disco in London!'

3

• Students read the text again and underline the connecting words and phrases. Feedback with reference to the text.

Answers

also (line 6)
then (line 7)
in the evening (line 11)
after that (line 9)
of course (line 2)
finally (line 11)
later on (line 6)

4

• Students replace the underlined expressions with appropriate connectors from exercise 3. Feedback.

Answers

1 Then/After that/Later on
2 Of course
3 In the evening
4 also
5 After that/Then

5

• Explain to students that they are going to write about their own perfect day. Students look at the photographs on page 55 and decide which of the activities they would like to do in their perfect day. In pairs, students brainstorm ideas and make notes under each photo.

• Students think of other things/places to include in their perfect day.

• Students work in pairs and answer the questions on the plan. Point out that these notes will help to make their article interesting and cohesive.

• Assign the article as homework. Remind students to use the plan, the notes and vocabulary and grammar in this unit. Point out that students should use the model on page 55 as a guide.

• In the next lesson, students exchange and read articles. Students decide if they like their partner's perfect day and make any corrections or changes they think necessary.

• Mark the articles and set a time limit in a subsequent lesson for feedback.

Sample article (126 words)

My perfect day would begin with a trip to Disneyland in Florida. Of course I would have breakfast in the best restaurant. There would be no one else there so I wouldn't have to wait for any of the rides. Also all of the rides would be free so I could go on them as many times as I wanted to.

After that I would fly to New York for lunch at the top of the Empire State Building. Then I would meet my friends and we would go to Sony and use their Play Station 2 all afternoon.

In the evening we would all fly to Italy to eat ice cream.
Finally my perfect day would end on a Greek island, swimming in the sea.

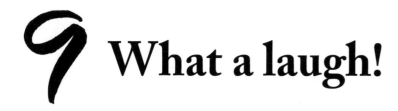

What a laugh!

Topics
Humour, embarrassing situations

Grammar
Third conditional, *wish* and *if only*

Vocabulary
Word formation, colours

Reading
'Humour is an international language':
gapped text

Listening
Four speakers describing embarrassing
moments: multiple matching

Speaking
Information gap (jokes)
Describing pictures

Writing
Narrative composition (short story
describing an embarrassing day)

Reading (pages 56–57)

☆ Text notes

• John Smith is the most common English name. The
British do not have a good reputation as foreign
language learners.

• Croissants are a common part of a continental
breakfast with coffee.

• Coco-pops are a chocolate-flavoured breakfast cereal.

• *Bon appétit* is what French people say before starting
a meal. In Britain it is normal to start eating your meal
without saying anything.

Warm up: establish the topic of the text by asking
students what languages they speak. Elicit what French
people might say as they begin to eat their meal (Bon
Appétit!). Ask if anybody knows similar expressions in
other languages (Spanish 'Que Aproveche!', Italian
'Buon appetito!', German 'Guten Apetit').

• In groups, students discuss which nationality they
think learns languages best. Feedback briefly.

1

• Students read the text quickly and answer the
questions. Set a time limit. Feedback.

Answers
1 John Smith, an English teacher/Madame Pompidou, a
French colleague
2 In Paris/at a conference/in a hotel
3 English/French

2

• Point out the numbers 1–5 in the text. Explain that
these numbers mark the position of missing sentences.

• Students read sentences A-E carefully and underline
key words which will help them to put the sentences
back into the correct place in the text.

• Students work alone or in pairs. They read each
paragraph carefully, focusing on the space where a
sentence is missing. Point out that they should read
what comes before and after the space to find
connections with the missing sentences. Feedback,
eliciting which words helped students decide where
the sentences go.

Answers
1 E (see previous sentence: he didn't speak any foreign
languages, line 10)
2 B (see reference to 'Conferences' in 'nice hotels' in
previous sentence)
3 D (see 'looked' in previous sentence and 'he had no
idea' in the next sentence)
4 C (see 'good food was very important in French
culture.' in the previous sentence)
5 A (see 'smiled'/'strong English accent' in previous
sentence)

3

• Students read the definitions and in pairs guess
which words match them. Students check their guesses
by reading the text again. Point out that the words are
given in the order in which they appear in the text.
Students underline the words as they find them in
the text. Feedback with reference to the text.

Answers
1 attended (line 11)   4 determined (line 37)
2 staff (line 15)   5 nodded (line 40)
3 colleague (line 20)

Third conditional
Grammar box

Direct students' attention to the grammar box on page 57. Students read the example.

• Check students understand by eliciting whether the example refers to the past, present or future. Elicit which conditionals refer to the present and future.

1

• Students read the text again to find and underline the example of the third conditional. Write it on the board.

If he had studied French harder at school, he would have understood her.

• Ask the following concept questions:

Did John Smith study French at school? (Yes)
Did he study hard? (No)
Did he understand the woman? (No)
Does he wish he had studied harder? (Yes)
Why does he wish he had studied harder? (because he would have understood the woman)

• Elicit which tenses we use with the third conditional and underline them in the example on the board (past perfect + *would have done*).

2

• Students work in pairs and complete the sentences. Feedback.

Answers
1 had had enough
2 had been less traffic
3 would have been able to
4 had not been in
5 wouldn't have lost
6 had been better
7 wouldn't have eaten

3

• Students complete the sentences, according to their interests and experiences. When students have written their sentences they should read them to each other. Feedback.

Speaking (page 58)

Warm up: write the following joke on the board, marking the stress:

Man: Darling, you <u>know</u> I love you. I would <u>die</u> for you!
Woman: You always <u>say</u> that but you never <u>do</u> it.

• Read it to the students. Ask the following questions to make sure they understand it:

What does 'it' refer to in the second line? (die)
Does the man really mean he would die for her? (no)

1

• Explain that students are going to work in pairs to tell each other simple jokes in English. Ask student A to turn to page 104 and student B to turn to page 113.

• Explain that student A has the first half of a joke and student B has the second half. Tell students to look through their sentences and make sure they understand them. Check the following items:

call (to name, to ask for, to call someone by a bad name)
false teeth (teeth that old people usually have when they lose their own teeth)
come out (appear, are removed)
bright (very clever, having lots of light)

• Explain that students must only look at their own sentences. Student A begins by asking a question, student B looks down his or her list of answers and chooses which he/she thinks is the correct one. If the answer to the question is correct, students have made a joke. Do the first one as an example:

Student A: Can you call me a taxi, please?
Student B: Certainly, sir. You're a taxi.

Answers
2 Why are false teeth like stars?
  Because they come out at night.
3 Why did the teacher wear sunglasses?
  Because her pupils were very bright.
4 What do you call a policeman with a banana in each ear?
  Anything you like, because he can't hear you.

2

• Direct students to the pictures on page 58. In groups students brainstorm what they can see. Feedback briefly.

• Students check the meaning of the words in the box. Focus on the following items:

graduate (v) to complete your studies at university and get your degree
vet is a doctor for animals
lion tamer is someone who can control a lion
whip is a long piece of wood and/or a piece of leather used for hitting animals or people. A lion tamer usually holds a whip.
canoe is a kind of boat which you sail on a river; you make it move by using one or two paddles.
paddle is a kind of flat piece of wood which you push in the water to make a canoe move
journal is a kind of diary
lion cub is a young lion

- Students work in pairs and tell the story of the woman's life using pictures 1–4 and the words in the box. Feedback, writing their sentences on the board.

- Direct students to pictures 5–8. Explain that this is what her life would have been like if she had done different things. Focus on the examples on the board. Ask a student to make a third conditional sentence from one of the examples:

If she hadn't gone to college, she would have been a lion tamer.

- Students work in pairs and talk about what would have happened to the woman if she had done different things, using pictures 5–8 and the words in the box. Remind students to use the third conditional. Feedback.

Suggested answers

If she had become a lion tamer, she would have had a more exciting life.
If she had joined the circus, she would have become a lion tamer.
If she hadn't gone to college, she would have joined the circus/become a lion tamer.
If she hadn't joined the circus, she wouldn't have gone to Africa.
She would have gone to Africa if she hadn't become a vet.
If she hadn't become a vet, she would have become a lion tamer.
If she had gone to Africa, she would have paddled down a river in a canoe.

Early finishers

- Early finishers should write as many third conditional sentences as they can about the woman.

Vocabulary 1 (page 58)

Word formation

1

- Write *happy* on the board and elicit from students words and phrases which derive from this word. Explain that they can make adjectives, adverbs, nouns and verbs.

- Elicit the words in the diagram.

- Students look at the diagram and identify which part of speech each word is. Feedback.

Answers

happy (adjective) happily (adverb) happiest (superlative adjective) unhappily (adverb) unhappy (adjective) happiness (abstract noun)

- Repeat with *laugh*. Feedback.

Answers

laugh (verb)   laughter (noun)   laughingly (adverb) laughable (adjective)   laughed (past simple, past participle)   laughing (present participle, adjective)

2

- Before students complete the sentences, they skim through them and decide which key word each one uses: *happy* or *laugh*. Feedback.

- In pairs or individually, students complete the sentences with an appropriate form of *happy* or *laugh*.

Answers

1 laugh	5 unhappy
2 laughing	6 happiness
3 happily	7 laugh
4 laughter	8 happy

3

- Students complete the sentences.

- When students have completed their sentences, they read them to each other. Feedback, by asking one or two students to tell the class what they have learnt about their partner.

Listening (page 59)

Warm up: establish the topic by writing *embarrass* on the board and asking if anyone knows what it means (to feel ashamed or silly in public).

- Ask the following concept questions to make sure they understand:

What happens to your face when you are embarrassed? (it goes red and hot)
Do you feel good or bad? (bad)

- Remind students of what they did with *happy* and *laugh* in the vocabulary section. In pairs, students brainstorm words using *embarrass*.

1

- Explain that in preparation for the listening exercise, students are going to check the meaning of some words. Provide these definitions for students to match with the words in the box:

someone who knocks things over or drops things (clumsy)
you tie your shoes with it (shoelace)
to make a short sound instead of talking (grunt)
to look at someone for a long time (stare)
to get into a position where you cannot move (stuck)
to save someone from a dangerous or difficult situation (rescue)

to disagree with something often by marching in the streets
(protest)
*a large piece of cardboard with a written message, often held
by people protesting in the streets* (placard)

2

• Students look at the pictures and in pairs describe what they see. Elicit:

a   A teenage girl has tried to climb through a window on the ground floor at the back of a house, but is stuck halfway. Group of neighbours standing around pointing and laughing.

b   Scene outside a shampoo factory – group of teenagers carrying placards and banners; they are protesting against the abuse of animal rights. They look puzzled. The factory does not look very busy.

c   Scene at a bowling alley. A teenage boy has run forward and fallen over his shoelaces flat on his face.

d   Scene at the zoo, outside the gorilla cage. Small tour bus, lots of tourists on board taking pictures. There is a family standing in front of the gorilla cage. Dad jumping up and down pretending to be a gorilla. Son looking very embarrassed.

• Students look at the pictures again and predict what each speaker is going to say about their embarrassing experience. Do not confirm any of the predictions yet.

• Explain that students are going to listen to four speakers and must match the pictures with the stories.

• Play the tape. Feedback.

Answers

1	c	3	b
2	d	4	a

3

• In this second listening, students listen for more detailed information. Students read the questions. Make sure they understand them and have a clear idea of what they are listening for. Students can try to remember who did what before they listen.

• Students listen to confirm who did what. Feedback, asking students to try and recall what each speaker said (see tapescript).

Answers

A	Speaker 3	D	Speaker 2
B	Speaker 1	E	Speaker 3
C	Speaker 4	F	Speaker 1

Tapescript (exercises 2 and 3)

SPEAKER 1: I sometimes wish I wasn't so clumsy. <u>For my thirteenth birthday</u> **(question 3 F)** I went bowling with my friends. On my last go all I needed to win was ten points, so I ran forward in those strange bowling shoes you have to wear. I hadn't noticed that my shoelace was untied and I tripped and fell on my face. Everyone was staring at me and <u>my friends were killing themselves laughing.</u> **(question 3, B)** If only I hadn't made such a fool of myself in front of everyone!

SPEAKER 2: I was visiting the zoo with my family when we stopped to have a rest and eat some ice-cream. Just then a tour bus full of tourists slowed down beside us. The tour guide in the bus was talking into the microphone. He said something like 'Over to the right you can see the gorillas,' and he pointed behind us. Suddenly, my dad stood up and started acting like a monkey, grunting like a huge gorilla, 'uh, uh' – you know. Everyone in the bus was just staring at us. I <u>was so embarrassed I could have died! I wish my dad wouldn't behave like a twelve-year-old all the time.</u> **(question 3, D)**

SPEAKER 3: Well, some friends and I decided we wanted to take action against products being tested on animals, so we spent hours and hours making signs that said things like 'Stop Testing on Animals Now' and 'Ban Cruelty to Animals'. <u>It took us all weekend to make them.</u> **(question 3, A)** Then we walked up and down outside a shampoo factory, holding these signs, until a woman came over and told <u>us the factory had closed down over two years before.</u> **(question 3, E)** You should have seen our faces! We wouldn't have made such fools of ourselves if we'd checked the facts first. Next time …

SPEAKER 4: One day my sister and I came home from school to find that we'd both lost our keys. One of the windows was open, so we decided to climb in that way. Debbie got in OK, but I ended up getting stuck because it was quite a small window. I just couldn't move. As if that wasn't bad enough, instead of Debbie coming to rescue me, she shouted to the neighbours for help. Soon there were five or six people laughing at me. <u>If only she'd kept her mouth shut!</u>
(question 3, C)

Optional activity

• Students can tell a partner about an experience they or somebody else found embarrassing.

Grammar 2 (page 59)

Wish and if only
Grammar box

Direct students to the grammar box on page 59. Students read the examples. Make sure they understand by asking these concept questions:

Can he/she speak a lot of languages? (No)
Would he/she like to? (Yes)
Did he/she study enough for the exam? (No)
Does he/she regret it? (Yes)
Does the neighbour play loud music? (Yes)
Does he/she like it? (No)
Will the neighbour turn it down? (No)

• Elicit some *wish* and *if only* sentences.

• Write them on the board. Elicit what stuctures follow *wish* and *if only*. Students check with the grammar box.

1
• Students complete the sentences in pairs.

Answers		
1 wasn't		2 had

2
• Students complete the sentences using the three structures that follow *wish/if only*. Feedback. encouraging students to give reasons for their answers.

Answers		
1 I were	4	they would not
2 I had studied	5	I didn't make
3 I were	6	you had been there/you had come

3
• Give students a couple of minutes to think about and write down their examples. If they find it difficult, point out that they can make something up.

• Students read their examples to their partner and use them as prompts for discussion.

Vocabulary 2 (page 60)

Colours
Warm up: in groups, students brainstorm colours.

• Students look at the pictures and identify the animals and the colours of each animal (a bright green lizard, a pale pink pig, a brilliant blue parrot, a dark brown horse, a jet black crow).

• Point out the use of *bright, pale, brilliant, dark* and *jet*. Remind students that we can only use *jet* with *black*.

Idioms
• Elicit the way we use these by asking these questions:

When do you go red as a beetroot? (when embarrassed)
When do you go white as a sheet? (when in shock or frightened)
What colour do you associate with envy or jealousy? (green)
If you feel cold, what colour are you? (blue)

1
• Students complete the sentences with the words given.

Answers		
1 sheet	5	blue
2 brilliant	6	red
3 black	7	pale
4 dark		

2
• Direct students to the picture on page 60. In pairs students quickly describe what they can see. Feedback focusing on the clothing.

• Students read the example. Make sure they understand what they have to do.

• Students describe what the people are wearing in more detail, adding colour expressions. Feedback, writing their sentences on the board.

Writing (pages 60–61)

Narrative composition
Warm up: elicit from students examples of embarrassing experiences that people (not themselves) may have. For example, falling over, saying something wrong, arriving very late for an appointment, being very clumsy, mistaking a stranger for a friend.

1
• This exercise focuses more specifically on embarrassing experiences the students may have had.

• Explain to students that they are going to interview a partner about embarrassing experiences.

• Students read the questionnaire. Make sure they understand each question.

• In pairs, students ask and answer questions beginning *Have you ever ...?* If their partner answers *Yes* the questioner writes their name next to the question. Direct students to the example by way of explanation. Feedback by asking one or two students to tell the rest of the class what they have found out.

• **Note:** If you suspect embarrassment may be caused, do not conduct feedback with the whole class.

2

• Students skim the text to answer the questions.

Answers
1 The writer is a student.
2 He/She had been to a party.
3 The alarm clock did not go off.
4 Because everybody looks at you as if you were a UFO.
5 When he/she came bottom in the maths test.

3

• Students read the expressions. Make sure they understand them by asking these questions:

Which expression starts a story? (it all began)
Which refers to the past? (the night before)
Which refers to the future? (the next day)

• Students complete the text with the expressions. Point out that students will need to read around each gap to make sure that they use the correct expression. Feedback with reference to the text.

Answers
1 The night before   3 By the time
2 It all began   4 The next day

4

• Students read the text again and label the paragraphs using the notes. Feedback, with reference to the text.

Answers
1 'I remember a day ... I wish I had stayed in bed'
2 'The night before, I had been to a party ... instead'
3 'Anyway ... soaking wet'
4 'Everybody was already ... everything'
5 'The next day ... day of my life'

5

• Students read the text again and underline examples of the tenses. Feedback with reference to the text.

Answers
1 **Past simple:** was a disaster, didn't go off, missed, got to school, said, laughed, were, went, sat, wrote, made, told, was
2 **Past perfect:** had stayed, had been, had come, had not gone, had done, had been
3 **Past continuous:** was pouring, was taking, was dripping

6

• Students work in pairs and try to complete the idiomatic expressions without looking at the text.

• Students check their answers by reading the text. Feedback.

Answers
1 pouring   3 million
2 soaking   4 mess

7

• Explain that students are going to write a story ending with the words: *If I had stayed home that day, none of this would have happened.* Elicit from students which tenses they are going to use most and why (past simple, past perfect, past continuous).

• Students read the instructions.

• Direct students to the expressions in the box and to the plan.

• Give them some time to decide what experience they are going to write about. Point out that they can make one up if necessary.

• Assign the story as homework. Remind students to use the plan, the grammar and expressions in this unit and the model as a guide.

• In the next lesson students exchange and read stories making corrections and changes if necessary.

• Mark the stories. Set a time limit in another lesson for feedback.

Sample composition (178 words)

It was Saturday morning. I had been at home all morning and I was bored. I decided go for a ride on my bike. I wanted to do some shopping anyway.

It all began when I was halfway down the road. It started pouring with rain. I got soaking wet, but I didn't turn back.

The roads were very wet and slippery. Suddenly, the bike skidded and I fell off. I felt really embarrassed, because a lot of people were watching me.

Just then, a car came up behind me and ran right over my bike. 'Stop!' I shouted to the driver, but he didn't! I was safe, but my bike was ruined and my clothes were dripping. A huge crowd was standing around me and I had gone red as a beetroot. I wished I had been a million miles away.

I had to walk home in the rain. It took an hour. So here I am in bed with a bad cold. If only I had stayed home that day, none of this would have happened.

Revision (Units 7–9)

Answers

1
1. have
2. could
3. have
4. of
5. would
6. of
7. have
8. feel
9. go
10. have
11. only

2
1. may be rain
2. has to wear
3. I would not
4. you don't leave me
5. she had seen
6. can't be
7. must be Jenny's letter

3
1. A
2. C
3. D
4. C
5. A

4
1. electrician c
2. recycle d
3. guitar e
4. laugh f
5. factory a
6. pollution b

5
1. d
2. g
3. a
4. e
5. b
6. c
7. f

6
1. ✓
2. the
3. for
4. ✓
5. ✓
6. to
7. for
8. of
9. do
10. ✓
11. ✓
12. other

Song

If I Could Turn Back Time

1 🔲

• Students listen to the song and answer the questions. Feedback.

Answers
1. hurting someone, saying something
2. lonely, sad

2

• Students match the words in list A with the meanings in list B. Feedback.

Answers
1	c	5	f
2	d	6	e
3	g	7	b
4	a		

3 🔲

• Students listen to the song again and number the words in exercise 2 in the order they hear them. Feedback.

Answers
1. weapon
2. wound
3. shattered
4. torn apart
5. swore
6. proud
7. blind

If I Could Turn Back Time

If I could turn back time
If I could find a way
I'd take back those words that have
    hurt you and you'd stay

I don't know why I did the things I did
I don't know why I said the things I
    said
Pride's like a knife, it can cut deep
    inside
Words are like weapons, they wound
    sometimes
I didn't really mean to hurt you
I didn't wanna see you go
I know I made you cry but, baby

If I could turn back time
If I could find a way
I'd take back those words that have
    hurt you and you'd stay
If I could reach the stars
I'd give them all to you
Then you'd love me, love me, like you
    used to do
If I could turn back time

My world was shattered, I was torn
    apart
Like someone took a knife and drove it
    deep in my heart
When you walked out that door I swore
    that I didn't care
But I lost everything, darling, then and
    there
Too strong to tell you I was sorry
Too proud to tell you I was wrong
I know that I was blind
and, darling …

CHORUS
If I could turn back time
If I could find a way
I'd take back those words that have
    hurt you and you'd stay
If I could reach the stars
I'd give them all to you
Then you'd love me, love me, like you
    used to do
If I could turn back time
If I could turn back time
Oh, baby

I didn't really mean to hurt you
I didn't wanna see you go
I know I made you cry but oh …

CHORUS
If I could turn back time
If I could find a way
I'd take back those words that have
    hurt you
If I could reach the stars
I'd give them all to you
Then you'd love me, love me, like you
    used to do
If I could turn back time
If I could find a way
I'd take back those words that have
    hurt you and you'd stay
If I could turn back time

Photocopiable

10 A question of difference

Topics
A real-life jungle boy, Tarzan, left-handed/right-handed people, cosmetic surgery, the Maya of Mexico

Grammar
The passive, the causative

Vocabulary
Collective nouns, arts and sciences

Reading
'Jungle Boy': multiple matching (headings)

Listening
Talk show about being left-handed: blank filling

Speaking
Information gap (spot the difference)

Writing
Project (an ancient civilization)

Reading (pages 64–65)

☆ Text notes

• This is a true story of a young boy brought up by monkeys who later rejoined human society. The boy developed the ability to communicate with monkeys and was the subject of a BBC documentary.

• Uganda is a country in East Central Africa. Its capital is Kampala. The population is made up of 18 different tribes but half of the people belong to the Bantu tribe.

• Mowgli is a character in *The Jungle Book,* a story by Rudyard Kipling. Mowgli is lost in the jungle from an early age and is brought up by wild animals.

• Tarzan is a character in stories originally written by Edgar Rice Burroughs. Tarzan was brought up from an early age by monkeys. His companion in the jungle is a woman called Jane. He is famous for having said to Jane: 'Me Tarzan, you Jane'.

• BBC stands for the British Broadcasting Corporation. It is a state-owned radio and TV company in Britain. It has a reputation for quality and reliability.

Warm up: use the photograph on page 64 to establish the topic of the text. Students work in groups and discuss what they think the text is going to be about. Feedback briefly.

1

• Students read the true/false statements and try to predict the answers.

• Students read the article quickly to check their predictions. Advise them to underline the part of the article where they find the answer. Feedback, with reference to specific points in the article.

Answers
1 True (line 1 and line 10)
2 False (line 2, lines 12–13)
3 True (line 56) (Accept false as an answer, if students say 'monkey language' is not a real foreign language)
4 True (lines 57–58)

2

• Students read the headings A–F. Check they understand them.

• Students read the article again and choose the correct heading for each paragraph. Point out that they do not need one of the headings.

• Students check their answers in pairs. Feedback with reference to the part of the article that helped students make their choice.

Answers
1	C	4	F
2	D	5	A
3	E	B	is not used

Optional activity

• Students discuss what they found most amazing about this story.

3

• Students find and underline the given words in the article. Feedback with reference to the article.

Answers
adopted (line 12)	realized (line 30)
came up to (line 21)	speechless (line 53)
chattered (line 25)	

• Students work in pairs and match the words with the definitions. Remind them to refer to the article for context.

Answers
1	came up to	4	chattered
2	speechless	5	adopted
3	realized		

Grammar 1 (page 65)

The passive

Presentation: write these questions on the board (they all use the passive voice):

Where was the jungle boy brought up?
Who was he brought up by?
Who was he discovered by?
Who was he adopted by?

• Elicit answers from students and write them on the board. They can refer to the article if they need to. Underline the passive in each answer.

The jungle boy <u>was brought up</u> in the jungle.
He <u>was brought up</u> by monkeys.
He <u>was discovered</u> by the woman collecting firewood.
He <u>was adopted</u> by monkeys/Pat and Molly Wassuna.

Grammar box

• Direct students to the grammar box on page 65. Check students understand by asking them to transform the passive sentences into active ones.

Answers
The police arrested the murderer.
Someone broke the window yesterday.
Pour the liquid into the jar and heat the mixture to 69°C.

• Make sure students understand the difference between the active and passive forms of the verbs, pointing out the key features.

1

• Students complete the sentences from the article. Students check their answers with the text. Feedback, focusing on the correct use of the passive.

Answers
1 Now a real life Mowgli <u>has been discovered</u>.
2 He <u>is called</u> John Ssabunnya.
3 When he was five or six years old he <u>was adopted</u> by monkeys.

2

• Students rewrite the sentences using the passive form. Feedback asking appropriate concept questions (in brackets).

Answers
1 My bike has been stolen! (Do we know who stole it?)
2 He was given a good mark for his composition by the teacher. (Is it obvious who gave the mark?)
3 Several different plants are taken to be analyzed. (Are we interested in the people or the process?)
4 The new office block will be finished by the New Year. (Do we know who will finish it? Is it important who will finish it?)
5 All children are taught to read and write. (Is it obvious who does the teaching?)
6 A film was made of the book by Hollywood. (Do we know the name of the director? What are we most interested in – the making of the film or who made it?)
7 The Tarzan books have been read by millions of people. (Is it obvious who reads them?)

3

• Elicit from students what they know about Tarzan.

• Students read the text quickly to see if any of their ideas are in the text.

• Remind students that they should read the whole text before completing it. This will make it easier.

• Students complete the gaps with the correct form of the verbs.

Answers
1	was created	7	is called
2	was published	8	were made
3	had been employed	9	have also been written
4	was made	10	have been translated
5	is/was brought up	11	will be made
6	is/was taught	12	will probably be directed

Listening (page 66)

☆ Text notes

• Being left-handed was thought to be bad. The word *sinister* which means *bad*, comes from the Latin for *left*.

• Hercules (Heracles in Greek) had superhuman strength. He carried out the twelve labours of Hercules and became immortal.

Warm up: use the photographs on page 66 to establish the topic of the listening. In pairs, students try to guess what the people have in common. Feedback briefly.

Answers
1 Alexander the Great, Macedonian Greek general and Emperor
2 Pete Sampras, Greek American tennis player
3 Leonardo de Vinci
4 George Michael, pop singer

1

• Students work in pairs and discuss which of the people is not left-handed. Feedback.

Answer
Pete Sampras

Optional activity

• You may wish to elicit other famous left-handed people: Einstein, Aristotle, Bruce Willis.

2 ▱

• Students read the sentences and complete them with *left* or *right*. Encourage students to guess if they do not know the answer. Feedback.

• Students listen to the tape and check their answers. Feedback.

Answers
1 right	5 right
2 left	4 right
3 left	6 right

3

• Establish who in the class is left-handed.

• Students copy the sentences into their notebooks using the hand they do not usually write with.

• Feedback on how difficult/easy students found it.

4 ▱

• Students listen to the tape and complete the sentences in exercise 3.

Answers
1 wrong
2 began
3 made

• Students discuss the question in pairs. Play the tape again for students to check their answers. Feedback, asking students to make specific reference to the listening text.

Answers
Speaker 1 'I was always told "don't use that hand" – it would always make me feel embarrassed.'
Speaker 2 'My problems began at school – my left-hand would cover the letters so I couldn't see them.'
Speaker 3 'things like scissors, corkscrews and doors ... very difficult ... I have to make sure I sit so that I don't push the person next to me.'

5 ▱

• Students read the sentences focusing on the underlined sections. Encourage them to guess what the speakers might have said.

• Students listen again and replace the underlined expressions with what the speakers actually say. Remember to pause the tape to give students time to write. Feedback.

Answers
1 feel embarrassed	4 problems
2 awkward	5 are very convenient
3 make comments	6 worked out

Tapescript (exercises 2, 4 and 5)

Part 1

PRESENTER

This week we look at some of the myths that have been associated with the left and right hand over the centuries. Later in the programme, we'll hear what some left-handed children have to say about life from a left-hand point of view.

But first, let's go back to Greek mythology. In ancient times, it was thought that the left side was the bad one. One story describes how Hercules, travelling along a road one day, came to a crossroads. Which way should he go – left or right? He thought for a moment and took the right-hand turning because the right was thought to be the side of truth and justice. (question 2, 1) This is still true in Europe today. Indeed, in some European languages, the words for 'left' and 'bad' are often the same or very similar. (question 2, 2)

In the Far East, however, things are sometimes the other way round. In China, for example, the left is the good side: it is the bright side and is more powerful than the right. (question 2, 3) If we turn to India, it is the right hand that is good, so presents are given with the right hand, which is believed to be the generous one. (question 2, 4, 5) Food is also eaten with the right hand. (question 2, 6) So things are not so simple. It all depends where you were born ...

Part 2

SPEAKER 1

Even before I went to school I remember that every time I waved to a friend of mine on the other side of the road, I was always told: 'No, don't use that hand (my left hand); use your good hand.' And it would always make me <u>feel embarrassed</u>. **(question 5, 1)** <u>I had no idea what was wrong with my left hand</u>. **(question 3, 1)** It was the same story every Sunday when I was taken to have lunch at my grandparents' house. My grandmother used to say, 'Hold your spoon with your right hand.' I did what I was told to do, but it made it much more <u>awkward</u> **(question 5, 2)** for me to eat.

SPEAKER 2
My parents never used to <u>make comments</u> **(question 5, 3)** about being left-handed. I was allowed to use my left hand because I felt more comfortable using that one. <u>My problems</u> **(question 5, 4)** <u>began at school</u>, **(question 3, 2)** when I had to learn to write for the first time. Everyone in my country writes from left to right across the page. If you're left-handed, it's not actually that easy. It's quite awkward, in fact. My left hand would cover the letters I was writing so I couldn't see them, and I kept making a mess of my writing. Later, I managed to find a way of solving that little problem.

SPEAKER 3
There are a whole lot of problems if you're left-handed because, let's face it, <u>the world is made for right-handed people</u>. **(question 3, 3)** Things like scissors, corkscrews and <u>doors are very convenient</u> **(question 5, 5)** for right-handed people and very difficult for left-handed types like me. When I sit down to eat at the table, I have to make sure I sit at one end, so that I don't push the person next to me with my elbow – other people are almost always right-handed. But I suppose it's not really such a big problem. Like most left-handers, I've <u>worked out</u> **(question 5, 6)** a way of surviving. People are quite adaptable, aren't they?

Vocabulary 1 (pages 66–67)

Collective nouns

Warm up: write this sentence from the reading text on the board and ask students to tell you the missing word:

A __ of woman were collecting firewood. (group)

• Elicit from students what other words they know like *group* which could go in the gap (crowd).

• Elicit words like *group* for animals (herd, flock).

1

• Students match the nouns in list A with the words and phrases in list B. Point out that often collective nouns are specific to a certain animal.

Answers

1	d	6	h
2	a	7	f
3	e	8	g
4	b	9	l
5	c		

• Elicit from students other words or phrases that could go with the collective nouns.

a pile of papers, a crew of people who work on a plane, a flock of sheep, a bunch of grapes/flowers, a swarm of flies/bees, a pack of wolves, a herd of horses/goats

2

• Students complete the sentences using collective nouns from exercise 1.

• Encourage students to try and complete the sentences without referring to exercise 1.

Answers

1	swarm	4	herd
2	bunch	5	flock
3	pile		

Speaking (page 67)

1

• This is an information-gap activity. Students describe two similar pictures in order to identify the differences. Explain to students that there are ten differences.

• Write this useful language on the board:
In my picture
…there is
…I can see
He is wearing…
He's got…

Answers

Jane's hair colour, monkey covering eyes, snake is a different colour, tail behind lion, gecko eating fly, bug on leaf, snake not rope, mouth open, parrot, leaves on plant on right

Grammar 2 (page 67)

The causative

Presentation: write the following sentences on the board:
I had my eyes tested yesterday.
I'm having my hair cut on Saturday.
They had the car fixed.
I was allowed to use my left hand.
You should have the roof repaired.

• Elicit which is the odd one out and why. (The odd one out is the fourth one. All the others are in the causative.)

• Elicit from students what they think the causative is and when it is used. (We use the causative when somebody else does something for us. We do not do it ourselves.)

• Check students understand by asking concept questions for some of the example sentences.

Did I test my eyes myself? (No)
Who did it for me? (the optician)
Am I going to take a pair of scissors and a mirror and cut my hair myself? (No)
Who is going to do it for me? (the hairdresser)

Grammar box

• Direct students to the grammar box on page 67. Make sure they understand how we form the causative in the following tenses:

Present simple: *I have my hair cut.*
Present continuous: *I'm having my hair cut.*
Past simple : *I had my hair cut.*
Future (*going to*): *I'm going to have my hair cut.*

1

• Direct students to the example.

• Students read the notes and in pairs decide which tense to use in each case.

• Students use the notes to make causative sentences. Feedback.

Answers
1 He has his suit cleaned once a month.
2 The old lady had her eyes tested last week.
3 I'm going to have my hair cut tomorrow.
4 We're having the house redecorated at the moment.
5 I haven't had my hair cut since last summer.

2

☆ Text notes

• Cher (1946–) is American. She is a popular solo singer and highly successful Hollywood actress. She is also well known for the plastic surgery she has undergone to keep her looking young and beautiful.

• Students work in pairs and discuss how Cher's appearance has changed. Elicit from students which they think is the most recent photograph.

3

• Students skim through the text to check their ideas in exercise 2.

• Students complete the text, using the passive or the causative. Encourage them to refer to the grammar boxes in this unit to avoid mistakes. Feedback, encouraging students to give reasons for their answers.

Answers
1 was born
2 was given
3 was made
4 had written
5 was given
6 made
7 has been transformed
8 has had her nose straightened
9 has had her hair styled

Vocabulary 2 (page 68)

Arts and sciences

Warm up: Students brainstorm the job titles they know.

1

• Students look at the headings and the words in the box.

• Check students understand the words in the box. Provide these definitions and ask students to match them with a word from the box:

a kind of tool used in science and medicine (instrument)
something written, a book before it is published (manuscript)
E = Mc² is a famous one (formulae)
what is left of classical sites or the remains of any building or town (ruins)

• Direct students to the example. Make sure they understand what they have to do.

• Students work in pairs to complete the lists with words from the box. Feedback.

Answers
1 painter, brush
2 sculpture, sculptor, statue
3 architecture, architect, building
4 science, scientist, formulae/instrument
5 mathematics, mathematician, formulae
6 astronomy, astronomer, telescope
7 archeology, archeologist, ruins
8 writing, writer/author, manuscript

Writing (pages 68–69)

Project

☆ Text notes

• The Maya were a native Mexican tribe who had a highly developed civilization. They worshipped gods and built pyramids to them. They were excellent painters and had a system of writing and mathematics.

• Egyptian civilization is one of the oldest in history. It dates from at least 2700 BC and saw the building of the great pyramids. The classic period of Egyptian art lasted from about 2000 to 1786 BC. Early Egyptians were ruled by powerful Pharoes.

• The Romans built an empire that lasted from about 50 BC till the 15th century in some areas. They were great law-makers and engineers.

• Students will be required to write about an ancient civilization (Greek, Egyptian, Roman). Encourage them to refer to encyclopaedias and the internet. They should find pictures connected with the topic. Ideally, they should present their project as a poster and stick the pictures on the poster. These posters could decorate the classroom.

Warm up: students brainstorm the names of ancient civilizations (The Greeks, the Chinese, the Phoenicians, the Egyptians, the Romans, the Aztecs, the Incas).

• Elicit what was special about them. Was it their art/their buildings/their religion/their laws?

1

• Students look at the photographs and identify which civilization they show (The Maya of Mexico).

• Students work in pairs and describe in detail what they can see in the photographs.

Answers

A Mayan pyramid, a Mayan sculpture

2

• Students complete the text using the passive phrases given. Students check their answers in pairs. Feedback.

Answers

1 are considered	4 were built
2 can still be seen	5 have been compared
3 was invented	6 is still produced

3

• Students read the text again and match the headings with the paragraphs. Feedback, by asking students to identify which parts of the text helped them to choose.

Answers

A Who were the Maya	D Art
B Science	E The Maya today
C Religion	

4

• Direct students to the ancient civilizations in the box. Students brainstorm what they know about them.

• Students label the photographs.

Answers

1 The Ancient Greeks	3 The Romans
2 The Ancient Egyptians	

5

• Students read the instructions. Make sure they understand what they have to do.

6

• Assign the project as homework. Remind students to use the paragraph plan, the expressions in the box and the grammar and vocabulary in this unit. Point out that students can use the text in exercise 2 as a model.

• In the next lesson students exchange and read projects making any necessary corrections or changes.

• Mark the projects. Students can then assemble their posters using the corrected text.

Sample project (170 words)

The Romans

The start of the Roman empire
The Romans were a powerful civilization who lived in Italy. Their empire reached from Great Britain to North Africa. It lasted from 27 BC until 476 BC. The city of Rome was founded much earlier, in 753 BC, by Romulus, who was its first king.

Science and art
The Romans invented central heating. Hot air was blown under the floors of their houses. They also loved baths and built public bath houses. They had long straight roads made by slaves to help their armies move quickly around the empire. The Romans made beautiful buildings, monuments, sculptures and mosaics.

Religion
The Romans believed in many gods and goddesses. These were often worshipped by making sacrifices in temples. They also believed their emperors were gods. For centuries they hated Christians and had them killed by wild animals in places like the Coliseum.

The Romans today
Rome was invaded by barbarians in the fifth century and its civilization came to an end. Today we can still see Roman villas, baths and roads. Films about the Romans, like 'Gladiator' are also very successful.

11 The fight for freedom

Topics
Nobel prize winners, Bob Marley, Amnesty International, Magic Johnson, Richard Gere, Nelson Mandela

Grammar
Relative clauses: *who, which, whose* and *that*
Relative clauses: *when* and *where*

Vocabulary
Nouns with and without the definite article
Noun suffixes

Reading
'Nobel women': multiple matching

Listening
Interview about Amnesty International: blank filling

Speaking
Pairwork task (discussing human rights)

Writing
Descriptive article (a person you admire)

Reading   (pages 70–71)

☆ Text notes

• Nobel, Alfred (1833–1896) was a Swedish engineer who invented dynamite and founded the Nobel Prize. He left his huge fortune to the Nobel Foundation to promote knowledge and peace.

• Aung San Suu Kyi (1945–) Burma. She was awarded the Nobel Peace Prize in 1991 for her peaceful struggle for democracy in her country. She studied philosophy, politics and economics at Oxford University.

• Rigoberta Menchu (1959–) Guatemala. She was awarded the Nobel Peace Prize in 1992 for her defence of the rights of the indigenous people of Latin America. She is a Mayan Indian. She had no formal education and worked as a maid for a wealthy white family as a young girl.

• Mother Theresa (1910–1998) She was awarded the Nobel Peace Prize in 1979. Mother Teresa was Albanian by birth. Her original name was Agnes Gonxha Bojaxhiu. In 1948, Mother Teresa became a citizen of India and took the name Teresa from a French nun, Thérèse Martin. Her initial work consisted of teaching the street children in Calcutta how to read. In 1950, Mother Teresa began to care for lepers and opened schools and homes for the poor and abandoned children.

• Bob Marley (1945–1981) was a Jamaican singer and songwriter. His songs were often about peace, freedom and social justice.

• Gandhi, Mahatma (1869–1948) India. He is famous for fighting for his country's independence using non-violent means. His philosophy of peaceful struggle has had an important influence on other civil rights campaigners such as Martin Luther King.

Warm up: Establish the topic of the text by asking students to read the title of the text and predicting what they think it is going to be about. Feedback briefly.

1

• Students brainstorm any Nobel Peace Prize winners they know. Elicit from students what they know about Bob Marley, Alfred Nobel and Gandhi. Elicit or give the information that they all fought for peace in different ways. Bob Marley through the words of his music, Nobel by founding the Peace Prize and Gandhi by using peaceful means to achieve political aims.

• Students read the texts to see which of the three names does not appear in the texts. Feedback.

Answer
Bob Marley

2

• Direct students to the photographs in the texts and elicit from students who they are and what they have in common.

Answers
A   Aung San Suu Kyi
B   Rigoberta Menchu
C   Mother Teresa
They have all won a Nobel Peace Prize; all women

• Students read the statements and in pairs try to match them with the women without referring to the text. Point out that the statements may refer to more than one person.

• Students read the text to check their answers. Advise them to underline the part of the text where they found the answers. Feedback.

3

• Students read the definitions and in pairs try to think of a word with a similar meaning without referring to the text.

• Students read the text again to check their answers. Feedback with reference to the text.

Answers

1 award (line 16)
2 ceremony (line 14)
3 chairperson (line 15)
4 struggle (line 11)
5 embassy (line30)
6 slums (line 41)

Grammar 1 (page 71)

Relative clauses: *who, which, whose, that*

Presentation: Write this sentence on the board and ask students to fill in the missing word:
The Nobel Peace Prize, _____ was founded in 1901 by Alfred Nobel, has been awarded to nine women.

• Elicit *which*.

• Write this sentence on the board and ask students to fill in the missing word:
Her father, _____ was the national leader, was assassinated.

• Elicit *who*.

• Elicit from students why we use *which* and *who* (to provide additional information about the subject; *which* for things and *who* for people).

Grammar box

• Direct students to the grammar box on page 71. Elicit from students which relative pronoun they have not discussed yet (*whose*). Elicit from them some examples of how it is used.

• Explain that where there are no commas, the relative clause is defining, provides essential information and cannot be removed. Where there are commas, the relative clause is non-defining, does not provide essential information and can be removed so that the rest of the sentence still sounds correct.

1

• Students read the text again and find and underline sentences containing *who, which, that, where* or *whose*.

• Feedback, encouraging students to tell you the subject that they are providing more information about.

Answers

The Nobel Peace Prize, which was founded ... (line 1)
Her father, who was ... (line 7)
... we depend on people who (line17)
people who can symbolize ... (line 18)
Aung San Suu Kyi is just such a person who fought ... (line 19)
woman in Guatemala, which is her ... (line 27)
... the embassy where the poor ... (line 30)
social work for her people, which is the reason (line 33)
in India where, at the age of 18 ... (line 38)
... the Missionaries of Charity, which aimed ... (line 42)

• Students identify which sentences use relative clauses to give information about people, things or ideas and places. Feedback.

2

• Students choose the correct relative pronoun, using the information in the grammar box to help them if necessary. Feedback, eliciting why the particular relative pronoun is appropriate in each case.

Answers

1 which (Stockholm is a place)
2 which (Russia is a place)
3 which (this refers to the whole of the previous clause)
4 which (nitro-glycerine is a thing)
5 whose (Nobel is a person and this is a possessive relative pronoun)
6 who (the relative pronoun refers to 'man')

Early finishers

• Early finishers complete the following sentences:
1 My neighbour, _____ son is a doctor, is a very useful person to have next door. (whose, non-defining)
2 People _____ live in glass houses should not throw stones. (who, defining)
3 The car _____ crashed has been taken away. (which, defining)

3

• Students complete the sentences with *who, whose* or *which*. Students check their answers in pairs. Feedback, encouraging students to give reasons for their answers.

Answers

1 which   4 who
2 who   5 who
3 whose   6 which

Listening (page 72)

☆ Text note

• Amnesty International was founded in 1961 to defend the human rights of prisoners and to fight other violations of human rights in countries all around the world. Its work has saved many lives and earned freedom for many people.

1 ▭

• These questions prepare students for the interview with a representative of Amnesty International that follows. Set a time limit for each question. Students work in pairs. Feedback briefly.

• Students listen and check their answers.

Answers

1 Peter Benenson founded Amnesty International in 1961 to defend people who had been imprisoned for their beliefs. In 1977 it was awarded the Nobel Peace Prize. Amnesty International is an organization that depends on the subscriptions of its members, not on government subsidies.
2 Its logo or symbol is a lighted candle surrounded by barbed wire (4).

2

• Explain to students that before they listen again, they are going to check the meaning of some words.

• Write these words on the board:
founder (verb *found*)
prisoner (verb *imprison*)
publicity (verb *publicize*)
subscription (verb *subscribe*)

• Elicit from students a definition for each word. Students check their answers by referring to page 72.

3 ▭

• Students read the notes. Make sure they understand them. Students can work in pairs to try and guess what words are missing before listening to the tape.

• Students listen to the tape and complete the notes.

Answers

1 1961	4 one million, 160
2 1962, four	5 hundreds
3 1977	6 no

Optional activity

• Discuss what students know about Amnesty International now that they did not know before.

Vocabulary 1 (page 72)

Nouns with and without the definite article

Warm up: write these incorrect sentences on the board and ask students to correct them:
The Nobel Peace Prize was founded by the Alfred Nobel.
Aung San was born in the Burma.
Aung San was in the prison.
(All of the sentences have an extra definite article.)

• Elicit from students why the article is not needed. Direct them to the explanations in exercise 1 if they have difficulty.

1

• Students read the sentences and in pairs discuss the differences between them. Feedback.

> **Answers**
> Without a definite article, *school* and *hospital* refer to the main purpose for which people go to *school* (as students) or *hospital* (as patients). The same applies to words like *prison* and *church*.
> If we say 'He's going to the school' or 'He is going to the hospital' we probably mean he is going to the place for another reason, apart from its main purpose, for example, to visit someone or because he has some kind of work there.

• Students read the examples and explanations on page 72. They should make a note of the common expressions with *home* and *work*.

2

• Students complete the sentences with the definite article or zero article. They should refer to the explanations and examples in exercise 1. Feedback, encouraging students to give reasons for their answers.

> **Answers**
> 1 the (the writer was not a patient)
> 2 — (the writer was a pupil)
> 3 — (the person referred to went to church as a believer)
> 4 the (the person referred to went to the church as an electrician)
> 5 the (the building is being used for a secondary purpose not its main purpose)
> 6 the (the noun is made specific)
> 7 — (fixed expression)

Speaking (page 73)

Warm up: introduce some of the concepts and useful language for the speaking exercise by asking these questions:

Have you read of countries where people are tortured?
Should people have the right to say what they like? In private? On TV? In the press?
How would you define democracy? Is it the right to vote? The right to choose?
Should men and woman get the same pay for the same job?
Should young people decide who to marry themselves or should their parents decide?

Useful language

• Students should give reasons for their decisions, using appropriate expressions. Before the discussion starts, you may like to write these on the board or elicit them from students:
I agree/disagree with this/I agree with you
I don't think so
I think
In my opinion
As far as I'm concerned
What's more
I'd also like to say
I think it's essential
I think it's important/more important

1

• Direct students to the pictures. Students work in pairs and describe what they see. Feedback briefly.

• Students read the statements and tell you what each one means.

• Students work individually and put the statements in order of importance to them.

• In pairs, students discuss each statement and explain why they have numbered them as they have.

• Encourage students to challenge their partner on their choices and to defend their own choices.

Early finishers

• Early finishers write down the five statements in their notebook and add their opinion of why each one is important.

Grammar 2 (page 73)

Relative clauses: *when* and *where*

Grammar box
Write these pairs of sentences on the board. Elicit from students how we can make them into one sentence:
I'll never forget that day. I met my best friend on that day.
(I'll never forget the day when I met my best friend.)
This is the building. I work there.
(This is the building where I work.)

• Direct students to the grammar box on page 73. They check their answers.

1

• Elicit from students what they know about Bob Marley.

• Students read the text quickly to see if any of the information they discussed is mentioned in the text.

• Explain to students that six relative pronouns are missing from the text. Direct students' attention to the example.

• Students work in pairs and decide where each relative pronoun should go. Feedback.

Answers

who married, where they lived, who were struggling, which was called, who had been, where his mother

2

• Explain to students that this exercise works in the opposite way. In this text there five extra relative pronouns. Students find them and cross them out.

Answers

which has its origins, which called, reputation who, when was warned, that never saw

Vocabulary 2 (page 74)

Noun suffixes

Warm up: write these words on the board:
music   murder

• Elicit from students which noun suffix to add to these words to describe what someone does (musi**cian**, murder**er**).

• Students brainstorm in groups other words which can be changed like this. Feedback.

1

• Students complete the list by adding a suffix. Feedback.

Answers

1	gangster	6	murderer
2	politician	7	blackmailer
3	celebrity	8	terrorist
4	musician	9	dictator
5	leader	10	student

Optional activity

• Check students understand the words by asking the following questions:
What do we call someone who is famous? (a celebrity)
What do we call someone who kills someone else deliberately? (a murderer)

What do we call someone who uses secret information about someone in order to make money? (a blackmailer)
What do we call someone who kills people to achieve political aims? (a terrorist)

2

• Students read the text quickly to find and underline any jobs mentioned (actors).

• Students read the text again and complete it using the correct form of the word given in capitals at the end of each line. Feedback.

Answers

1	newspapers	6	musicians
2	favourite	7	personal
3	personalities	8	celebrities
4	reporters	9	journalists
5	politicians	10	especially

• Students read the completed text to find more jobs.

Answers

reporter, musician, journalist

Writing (pages 74–75)

Descriptive article

☆ Text notes

• Magic Johnson, great American basketball player who, after he was diagnosed with AIDS, campaigned to inform people about the disease.

• Richard Gere, American actor (famous for the film Pretty Woman) and also campaigner for the rights of the people of Tibet.

• Nelson Mandela, ex-President of South Africa. He had served twenty-six years in prison before he was freed and became the leader of his country.

• Hilary Clinton, wife of ex-President Bill Clinton

1

• Students work in pairs and discuss which famous people they admire.

• Encourage students to challenge their partner's ideas and defend their own. Feedback.

2

• Students read the instructions. Make sure they understand what they have to do.

• Direct students to the photographs on page 74.

Students work in pairs and identify the famous people. Feedback.

• Students read the model text on page 75 to find which of the famous people in the photographs is not mentioned.

Answer

Hilary Clinton

3

• Elicit from the students that the paragraphs in the model text are in the wrong order.

• In pairs or individually, students read the text again and put the paragraphs in the correct order, underlining the words or phrases that helped them. Feedback.

Answer

Paragraph 1: <u>In my opinion</u>, there are ... (introduces the topic)
Paragraph 2: <u>Firstly,</u> in sport (gives example from sport)
Paragraph 3: <u>As for</u> show business (gives example from show business)
Paragraph 4: <u>Finally,</u> there are (gives example from politics)
Paragraph 5: <u>To sum up</u> (conclusion)

4

• Students label the five paragraphs using the notes. Feedback, encouraging students to give reasons for their answers. See answers to exercise 3.

5

• Direct students to the underlined words in the text.

• Students read the text again and replace the underlined words with the correct form of the alternatives given. Point out that by varying the vocabulary and avoiding repetition students can make their writing more interesting. Feedback.

Answers

a great deal
most outstanding/most popular/greatest
brilliant/outstanding
is sensitive to
great/brilliant/outstanding/popular
meaningful/outstanding
great/strong/popular

6

• Students find and underline the relative clauses in the model text.

Answers

Magic Johnson is someone who ...
helping people who ...
Gere is an actor who ...
is someone who cares about ...
who wrote good songs ...
songs which were ...
people who ...
a few politicians who ...

7

• Remind students of the discussion they had in exercise 1 about people they most admire.

• Direct them to the expressions given and remind them to use the grammar and vocabulary taught in this unit. Point out that students can use the model article in exercise 2 as a guide.

• Assign the article as homework.

• In the next lesson students exchange and read articles making corrections and changes if necessary.

• Mark the articles and set a time limit in another lesson for feedback.

Sample article (131 words)

The person I admire most is Nelson Mandela. Firstly I admire him because he is someone who has achieved outstanding success in politics in a country where life was very difficult for a great number of black people.

Nelson Mandela, who was in prison for twenty-six years, was a strong and popular leader of South Africa and has become an international hero. Another of his great qualities is his ability to talk to people. He is someone who people all over the world want to hear and listen to. Moreover, he is a good listener and is sensitive to people's needs. Finally I admire him because he continued to fight for freedom despite being in danger.

To sum up, Nelson Mandela is one of the most brilliant politicians of our time.

12 Life in the 21st century

Topics
Life in the future – androids, e-cinema

Grammar
Future perfect simple
Future continuous

Vocabulary
Phrasal verbs with *up*
Phrasal verbs

Reading
'Almost human?': multiple choice

Listening
Interview with a futurologist: true/false

Speaking
Discussion (life in the future)

Writing
E-mail message (describing future plans)

Reading (pages 76–77)

☆ Text notes

• Androids are robots that look like human beings and simulate some of the behaviour of human beings.

• MIT, the prestigious Massachusetts Institute of Technology

• NASA, the National Aeronautics and Space Administration, is the US centre for research into space which also organizes journeys of space exploration.

Warm up: direct the students to the photograph. Elicit from students what they think the text is going to be about. Ask them which jobs robots already do and what they might do in the future.

1

• Explain that in preparation for reading the text students are going to check the meaning of some words.

• Students work in pairs and try to guess what the correct word is for each definition.

2

• Students read the text to check their answers. Advise students to underline the words as they find them. Feedback with reference to the text.

Answers	
1 android (line 5)	4 Frankenstein (line 30)
2 humanoid (line 17)	5 micro-chip (line 35)
3 optimist (line 16)	6 gadget (line 37)

3

• Students read the beginning of each statement (not the possible endings) and find the part of the text that it refers to. Set a time limit. Students work in pairs.

Answers	
1 lines 7–10	4 lines 24–28
2 lines 13–14	5 lines 38–40
3 lines 16–18	

• Students read the possible endings for each statement, check back to where in the text they found the beginning of each one, read around that point and choose the best answer. Warn them that they should not expect the wording of the text to be the same as that of the answer, but that the meaning should be the same. Feedback with reference to the text.

Answers	
1 D	4 A
2 C	5 C
3 D	

Optional activity

• Students underline something in the text they agree with and something they disagree with.

• They show their sentences to their partner and explain why they chose them.

4

• Students read the definitions and try and guess which words they describe.

• Students read the text to check their answers. Point out that they have been given the last syllable of each of the missing words.

Grammar 1 (page 77)

Future perfect simple

Presentation: Elicit an example from the students by asking:
What time is it now?
What time does the lesson finish?
What time did it start?
How long will it have lasted by (nine) o'clock?

• Write the example on the board.
By (nine) o'clock, the lesson will have lasted (one hour).

Grammar box

Direct students to the grammar box on page 77. Students read the example and the explanation of how to use the future perfect simple. Check students understand by asking the following concept questions about the example:
Is it nine o'clock now? (No)
Is he/she doing homework? (Yes)
Has he/she finished? (No)
What time will he/she finish? (nine o'clock)

• Elicit from the students when the future perfect is used (when we talk about an action which will be completed between the moment of speaking and a specific time in the future).

1

• Students complete the sentences and then check their answers with the text:

Answers

1 will have made (lines 2–3)
2 will have created (lines 16–17)
3 have created (line 30)

2

• Students complete the sentences using the future perfect form of the verbs in brackets. Feedback.

Answers

1	will have disappeared	4	will have found
2	we will have found	5	will have killed
3	will have banned	6	will have become

3

• Students complete the sentences with their own ideas.

• In pairs, students discuss their sentences. Feedback.

Speaking (page 78)

Warm up: write the date *2050* on the board. Students brainstorm predictions about what will have changed by then.

• Elicit from students whether they are optimistic or pessimistic about the future.

1

• Direct students to the pictures on page 78. Students work in pairs and describe what they can see. Feedback briefly.

Answers

Picture 1 shows a very polluted, technical world.
Picture 2 shows a greener, gentler world.

• Students read the questions and the words in the box above the pictures. Make sure they understand them.

• Students work in pairs and discuss the pictures using the questions and the words in the box. Feedback, encouraging students to give reasons for their opinions.

Early finishers

• Early finishers can write down their answers to the questions.

Vocabulary 1 (page 78)

Phrasal verbs with *up*

Warm up: write *up* on the board and elicit from students any phrasal verbs they know with *up*.

• Build up a diagram on the board like the one on page 78. Add examples elicited from the students.

• Encourage students to make sentences showing different meanings for the phrasal verbs in the diagram.

pick up – I took a taxi from the station because no-one came to pick me up./The best way to learn a language is to pick it up from friends.

bring up – The children were brought up in the country and know the name of plants and flowers./She brought up the subject of money during the discussion.

turn up – In my country people always turn up late for meetings.

give up – I gave up playing football because I was too busy.

make up – She did not tell the truth – she made up the whole story./After they quarrelled they made up and became friends again.

show up – My dad made a silly joke in front of all my friends and really showed me up.

I

• Students complete the sentences with an appropriate phrasal verb from the diagram. Feedback.

Answers
1 give	4	turned/showed
2 turned/showed	5	brought
3 picked		

2

• Students work in pairs and replace the underlined words with phrasal verbs. Point out that students may have to change the form of the verb.

Answers
1 showed up	4	pick you up
2 turn up	5	brought up
3 made it up		

Listening (page 79)

☆ Text notes

• The title *Brave new world* comes from a famous novel about the future by Aldous Huxley in which the people live a comfortable life but with little freedom.

• Telecommuters are people who work from home for a company using a computer connected to the office of the company for which they work. Telecommuting is the name of this kind of work.

• Gene cards will be electronic 'smart' cards, like modern identity cards but containing information about the individual's genetic make-up.

• On-line education is based on the computer. The student is linked with teachers, students and sources of information through the internet and e-mail.

• Virtual classrooms will be classrooms based on the computer where contact with teachers, students and materials will be through the computer screen.

Warm up: establish the topic of the listening by asking students if they have heard of the novel *Brave new world*. Explain the gist of the novel and ask them if they agree that life in the future will be more controlled than it is today.

I

• Students read the questions and discuss them with a partner. Point out that it does not matter if they cannot answer them all. They can check their answers and listen for the ones they do not know when the tape is played.

2 ▣

• Students listen to the interview and check their answers to exercise 1. Feedback.

Answers
1 Working from home using a computer to link you with the office.
2 It causes less pollution and saves time.
3 It will contain genetic facts about people.
4 There will be fewer newspapers.
5 The use of computers to link the student with the teachers through e-mail and the internet.

3 ▣

• Students read the true/false statements. Point out that this time they will have to listen more carefully to find specific information.

• Students underline key words in each statement that will help them to find the information on the tape.

• Students listen again and decide whether the statements are true or false. Feedback.

Answers
1 False	5	True
2 True	6	False
3 False	7	False
4 True		

4

• Students work in pairs and make a list of the most important predictions made by the futurologist.

• Students discuss in pairs whether they think the predictions are correct.

Tapescript (exercises 2 and 3)

STUDENT 1: I'd like to ask you if we're going to have work when we leave school, because I've heard that in twenty years' time unemployment will be getting worse.

FUTUROLOGIST: Yes, of course, there'll be work in the future, but it'll be of a different kind. In the past, you know, most people used to go out to work every day by bus or car and <u>it took them a long time to get through the traffic. And a lot of pollution was caused as well, which was a big problem.</u> (question 1, 2) Well, <u>nowadays more and more people are working from home using their computers – this is called telecommuting (question 1, 1)</u> – and we'll be seeing <u>more and more people working from home in the</u>

future. (question 3, 1) People will be working fewer hours as well. We'll need people to work these computers, but we'll also need people to help us enjoy our free time. There will be more jobs in entertainment, sports and so on. Next question?

STUDENT 2: Are we going to get healthier – I read somewhere that we are all going to get fatter. Is that true?

FUTUROLOGIST: It's a good question. One disadvantage of working less, and working from home, is that people are getting less and less exercise. They're spending a lot of time sitting in front of the computer, and this is making them overweight. <u>Over the next few years, people will be getting fatter and fatter.</u> (question 3,2) This isn't a new problem. For the last two million years human beings have been getting more and more overweight. In 1950, twenty-five per cent of Americans were overweight; now about fifty per cent are. And I'm afraid this trend is going to continue. Perhaps by the year 2020 scientists will have found a simple, safe solution to weight control. <u>The pills that have been available up to now have on the whole been harmful to health.</u> (question 3,3) We'll have to wait and see, won't we?

As far as health in general is concerned, we will all have a personal gene card – just like we have a personal identity card now. <u>This personal genetic identity card will contain all the important genetic information about you from the moment you were born.</u> (question 1,3) <u>If you've got a health problem, you'll go to the doctor and show them your gene card. Then they'll tell you what treatment is best for you, using the information on your card.</u> (question 3,4)

STUDENT 3: Are there still going to be newspapers and books?

FUTUROLOGIST: I think we can expect big changes in the media – TV screens will get bigger and bigger, and electronic cinema or e-cinema will have become a part of our everyday life. As for newspapers, well, <u>ecologically speaking, they're bad news! We can't really afford to cut down any more trees, can we</u>? (question 1, 4)

One practical solution might be <u>an electronic newspaper about the size of an A4 sheet of paper. It'll be made of plastic and it'll have a tiny micro-chip inside, holding a huge amount of information.</u> (question 3, 5) It'll be much cleaner too. Wherever you are, when you want to read *The Times* or your favourite comic or sports magazine, you'll just take out your little plastic folder, press the chip and read. When you finish, you'll just close your little bit of plastic and put it back into your pocket. <u>So it looks as if we'll be cutting down fewer trees in the future</u> (question 1, 4, question 3, 6) – which I think is good news for the trees, don't you? One last question.

STUDENT 4: Will there still be schools?

FUTUROLOGIST: Well, <u>we're already seeing more and more virtual classrooms where computers link learners</u>

<u>and teachers from all over the world. I think we'll be seeing more and more of this on-line education in future.</u> (question 1, 5) Yes, I definitely think that's the way things are going, but <u>that doesn't mean there won't be any conventional schools at all. There'll simply be more ways of studying, whether you're learning at home</u> (question 3, 7) or in class. Thank you.

Grammar 2 (page 79)

Future continuous

Presentation: Elicit examples from students by saying:
On Saturday I will be seeing a friend of mine in the evening. What about you ? What will you be doing?

Grammar box
Direct students to the grammar box on page 79.

• Make sure students understand the example by asking these concept questions:
Do a lot of people work from home now? (No)
When will more people work from home? (In 20 years' time)

• Elicit examples of other things students think people will be doing in 20 years' time.

1

• Students read the reading text on page 76 to find and underline all the examples of the future continuous.

Answers
Robots like robonaut ... will be doing dangerous jobs (line 22)
They will also be doing more of the housework (lines 23–24)
more and more people will be wearing micro-computers (lines 33–34)
we will still be falling in love (line 39)

2

• Students read the title and try to guess what *E-cinema* means. Students read the text quickly to check their guesses. Feedback.

Answer
E-cinema will be cinema projected from a computer, not from the back of a room by a film projector, as at present. It means the quality of the film will always be the same, regardless of how old it is or where it is shown.

• Students read the text and choose the correct future form. Feedback, encouraging students to give reasons for their answers.

Answers

1 will see (simple future for prediction)
2 will still be going (process continuing at a specific point in the future)
3 won't be watching (process continuing at a point in the future)
4 will have come (completed action predicted for some point in the future)
5 will have (state not a process, therefore the continuous form is not appropriate)
6 will be using
7 will be doing

Vocabulary 2 (page 80)

Phrasal verbs

Warm up: elicit from students any examples of phrasal verbs with the following main verbs :
set   turn   get   find   carry

• Elicit example sentences from students.

1

• Students read the phrasal verbs in list A and the verbs in list B. Elicit from students which list is more informal (list A).

• Point out that phrasal verbs usually sound more informal than their one-word synonyms.

• Students match the phrasal verbs in list A with their synonyms in list B.

Answers

1	c	4	f
2	a	5	d
3	b	6	e

2

• Students work in pairs to complete the sentences with an appropriate phrasal verb from exercise 1.

Answers

1	carry on	4	setting off
2	find out	5	turned into
3	get away	6	get back

Writing (page 80)

E-mail message

Warm up: elicit from students some common phrases/expressions used in e-mails and chat rooms.

• Elicit from students if they are formal or informal.

• Write *slang* on the board and elicit from students what it means (idiomatic English).

• Explain that sometimes the English used in chat rooms is different from what students are used to in written English.

1

• Direct students to the expression box on page 80 and explain that these are typical examples of chat room language.

• Students read the examples and make a note of the main differences from standard English (for example, abbreviations – letters instead of words, the use of numbers (2, 4) avoiding capital letters, Americanisms (wanna), ellipsis (words missing – just thought)).

2

• Students work in pairs to write out the dialogue in full, correct English. Each student should only write out one of the parts, Sonia or Alex. Remind students to use the glossary in exercise 1 to help them. Feedback by asking one student to read Sonia and the other to read Alex.

Answer

Sonia:	Hey, how are you today stranger?
Alex:	Great, thanks! It's good to see you here again.
Sonia:	Me, too!
Alex:	I had a few things to do for school but I will have finished them by Friday.
Sonia:	Did you do well in that test on Monday?
Alex:	You bet. I worked like mad on it.
Sonia:	So what are you doing on Friday night then?
Alex:	Well, I'll be going to Jenny's party. Do you want to come?
Sonia:	You bet.
Alex:	Great. I'll pick you up at 9 o'clock at the usual place.
Sonia:	Thanks. Hey, will you be free to come to the club on Saturday?
Alex:	You bet.
Sonia:	With me I hope.
Alex:	Who else, stupid? But I'll be dropping in on my mate Manuel in hospital because he's having his tonsils out.
Sonia:	You don't say! You mean he's having an operation? Ugh!
Alex:	Yes, that's right. Not much fun.
Sonia:	I bet. When will you be going?
Alex:	Some time on Saturday morning. Hey, have you got the latest Mana CD?
Sonia:	You bet.
Alex:	Can you lend it to me because I want to make Manuel a copy. It will cheer him up. Thanks.

3

• Direct students to the highlighted words and expressions in the dialogue. Elicit from students whether these are formal or informal (informal).

- Students read the words and expressions in the list. Elicit whether these are formal or informal (formal).

- Students replace the words and phrases underlined in the dialogue with the words and expressions in the list.

Answers
Fine
very hard
would you like to
come and get you
stupid
visiting
friend
really?
make him feel happier

4

- Students read the text for gist to answer these questions:
What kind of message is this? (an e-mail)
Who is the writer? (Alex)
Who is he writing to? (Maria)
Do they know each other well? (Yes)
How is the writer going to spend his time in the next few days? (Jenny's party/visit a friend in hospital)

- Students complete the message with appropriate word or phrases.

- Remind students to use informal language. Feedback.

Answers
1 lots/a lot	6 having
2 will have	7 to buy/get
3 will	8 cheer him
4 be going	9 going out
5 drop in	

5

- Students complete the dialogue by answering the questions about themselves.

- Explain to students that they will be using their answers in their writing.

6

- Students write an e-mail message incorporating some of the information they wrote down in their answers to the dialogue in exercise 5. Remind them to keep the text informal, using contractions, phrasal verbs and other features of informality practised in this unit.

- Assign the message as homework.

- In the next lesson students exchange and read messages making any necessary corrections and changes.

- Mark the messages and set a time limit in another lesson for feedback.

Sample message (152 words)

Hi Mariana!

Thanks for your message. It was great to hear from you. Glad your trip went well. As for me, well, I'm fine. Things aren't too bad at all. I'm very busy with homework but I'll have finished by about 9 this evening. We've got a test on Monday so I've got to get some work done.

Anyway, when I've finished it all, I'm going out with Jenny. I'll need a break by then! I can't wait for the weekend to come. I've got to get on with my revision, so I'll be doing a lot of studying again, but I will have finished most of it by Saturday evening. Can't wait to get this test over. I'll be going to the cinema with my best friend. I haven't seen her for ages! We've both been so busy.

Anyway, that's all for now.

Take care

lots of love

Rosie

Revision (Units 10-12)

Answers

1
1. had
2. by
3. built
4. who
5. were
6. were
7. be
8. for
9. will
10. that/which
11. will
12. But

2
1. had my hair dyed
2. had the Pyramids built
3. when she was born
4. have a garage built
5. I'm having
6. we will have found
7. was smashed by

3
1. set off on
2. get back
3. found out
4. get away
5. turned into
6. carry on

4
1. give up
2. turned up
3. made up
4. brought up
5. picked it up
6. brought out

5
1. c
2. a
3. d
4. f
5. e
6. g
7. b

6
1. education
2. professions
3. architecture
4. mathematician
5. scientific
6. archeologist
7. historical
8. paintings
9. sculpture
10. examination

Song

The Miracle

1 🔊

• Check students understand *miracle*. Elicit examples of miracles.

• Students listen to the song and write down the two miracles the singer is still waiting for. Feedback.

Answers
1. an end to war/peace
2. freedom and an end to poverty

2 🔊

• Students read the list of miracles. Make sure they understand them by asking these check questions:

Which of these is a building? (Taj Mahal)
Which of these is a painting? (Mona Lisa)
Which was a famous pop star? (Jimi Hendrix)
Which of these is another expression for peace? (perfect harmony)
Are test-tube babies created naturally? (No)

• Students listen to the song again and number the miracles in the order they hear them. Feedback.

Answers
1. The Taj Mahal
2. Test-tube babies
3. The Hanging Gardens of Babylon
4. Jimi Hendrix
5. Perfect harmony
6. Sunday mornings
7. Mona Lisa

The Miracle

Every drop of rain that falls
In Saraha Desert says it all
It's a miracle
All God's creations great and small
The Golden Gate and the Taj Mahal
That's a miracle
Test-tube babies being born
Mothers, fathers dead and gone
It's a miracle
We're having a miracle on earth
Mother Nature does it all for us

The wonders of this world go on
The Hanging Gardens of Babylon
Captain Cook and Cain and Abel
Jimi Hendrix to the Tower of Babel
It's a miracle, it's a miracle, it's a
    miracle, it's a miracle

The one thing we're all waiting for
Is peace on earth, an end to war
It's a miracle we need – the miracle, the
    miracle
We're all waiting for today

If every leaf on every tree could tell a
    story
That would be a miracle
If every child on every street
Had clothes to wear and food to eat
That's a miracle
If all God's people could be free
To live in perfect harmony
It's a miracle
We're having a miracle on earth
Mother Nature does it all for us

Open hearts and surgery
Sunday mornings with a cup of tea
Super powers always fighting
But Mona Lisa just keeps on smiling
It's a miracle, it's a miracle, it's a
    miracle
It's a miracle, it's a miracle, it's a
    miracle, it's a miracle

The one thing we're all waiting for
Is peace on earth, an end to war
It's a miracle we need – the miracle, the
    miracle
Peace on earth, an end to war today

That time will come, one day you'll see
When we can all be friends
That time will come, one day you'll see
When we can all be friends
That time will come, one day you'll see
When we can all be friends

13 I spy...

Topics
James Bond films, Bond actors, spies

Grammar
Reported speech: tense changes
Reported speech: other changes

Vocabulary
Phrasal verbs with *take*
Narrative styles

Reading
'Their names were Bond': multiple matching

Listening
Extract from a 'Charles Pond' film: blank filling

Speaking
Describing photographs and discussion (violence in the media)

Writing
Narrative composition (short adventure story)

Reading (pages 84–85)

☆ Text notes

• The title of the text is based on the line made famous by James Bond who on introducing himself would say 'My name's Bond. James Bond.'

• *never says never* (line 1) – the title of one of the James Bond films was *Never Say Never Again*.

• James Bond (007), the fictional spy created by Ian Fleming, a British writer. The character became famous in the 1960s in films such as *Dr No* and *Goldfinger*. The Bond films were famous for their display of technology, comic-book violence and spectacular scenes of adventure.

• James Bond was first played by the Scottish actor, Sean Connery but has since been played by several different actors, including Roger Moore, George Lazenby, Timothy Dalton, David Niven and more recently Pierce Brosnan.

• Sean Connery (1930–), Scottish actor who became famous as James Bond. He has since appeared in the Indiana Jones films.

• Roger Moore (1927–), British actor who became famous as the *Saint* on television and James Bond in the cinema. He has also been active in work for the United Nations in support of poor children around the world.

• Pierce Brosnan (1953–), Irish actor who became famous for playing James Bond in the 1990s.

Warm up: write *007* on the board. Students tell you what they associate with the numbers (James Bond).

• Students brainstorm in groups how much they know about James Bond. Feedback briefly, eliciting information about: the character, the actors who played him, the films about him, their favourite Bond movies.

1

• Direct students to the photos on page 84. Students work in pairs and try to name the actors in the photos. Feedback briefly.

• Students discuss what the photos have in common (they are all photographs of actors who have played James bond in the cinema: Sean Connery, Roger Moore, Pierce Brosnan).

• Students discuss question 2 in pairs. Their answers will be personal opinion. Feedback.

2

• Students read the true/false statements and discuss their answers in pairs before they read the text.

• Students read the text quickly (skim) to check their answers. Set a time limit. Advise students to underline the part of the text where they find the answer. Feedback with specific reference to the text.

Answers
1 False ('British spy James Bond', line 1)
2 True ('1962's *Dr No*. This was the first film in a series.' line 11)
3 True ('They didn't use to have blood and brains spilled all over the place' line 27)
4 False ('Connery; 'the first actor to play superspy James Bond' lines 10–11)
5 True ('In 1995 he appeared in his first Bond movie' lines 33–34)

3

• This is a scanning exercise. Students will need to look for specific information in each text. Students quickly read the questions. Make sure they understand them.

• Set a time limit (no more than 10 minutes). Encourage students to look only for the information asked for and to make a note of the line(s) where the information is given. Point out that some actors can be chosen more than once.

• Students compare answers in pairs. Feedback with reference to the text.

Answers

1 B (lines 25–27)	5 A (lines 8–9)
2 C (lines 31–32)	6 B (lines 21–22)
3 C (line 29)	7 A (lines 14–15)
4 A (lines 13–14)	

4

• Students read the definitions and in pairs try and guess the words before they read the text again.

• Students check their answers with the text. Advise them to underline the part of the text where they find the word. Feedback with reference to the text.

Answers

1 deliver (line 5)	4 scenes (line 25)
2 producer (line 14)	5 stunts (line 35)
3 earn (line 22)	

Grammar 1 (page 85)

Reported speech: tense changes

Presentation: write the following on the board and ask students to complete the second of the sentences.

'I work as an actor.' He told them he ...
'I'm making a new film.' She said she was ...
'I've made six Bond films.' He told us he ...
'I played the countess in the film.' She said she ...
'I was making a film at the time.' The actress said she ...

Grammar box

• Direct students to the grammar box on page 85. Students read the chart of tense changes from direct to reported speech and check their answers to the above sentence completion exercise.

• Students complete the following chart of tense changes from direct to reported speech:
present simple ➜past simple
present continuous ➜
present perfect ➜
past simple➜ past perfect
past continuous ➜

• Students check their answers with the grammar box on page 85.

1

• Students read the interview for gist to answer these questions:
What job did B used to do? (a spy)
What was B's secret name? (Lola)
When did B become a spy? (in 1935)
Is B a man or a woman? (woman)

• Students complete the newspaper report using the appropriate reported speech forms and information from the interview. Feedback.

Answers

1 had been	6 had thought/believed
2 had	7 had
3 was staying	8 hadn't received
4 had been	9 had become
5 had given	

Optional activity

• Explain to students that the text is based on a true story. Initiate a class discussion using these questions:
What do you think of the old lady?
Why do people become spies?
Why do they give away their country's secrets?

Speaking (page 86)

Warm up: establish the topic of the speaking exercise by asking students: *Which of the James Bond actors thought the Bond films had become too violent?* (Roger Moore)

• Elicit from students whether they agree with him and how they feel generally about the amount of violence in films and on the television. Do not spend too long discussing these points.

1

• Direct students to the photos on page 86. Students work in pairs and describe what they see. Feedback and elicit whether there is any connection between them.

Suggested answer

They show how TV might cause young people to become violent. If they watch violence on TV young people may try to imitate the violence.

2

• Students read the interview questions and the box of useful expressions. Make sure they understand them by asking two confident students to demonstrate the exercise.

Student A asks a question.
Student B answers using direct speech and some of the expressions in the box.
Student A reports Student B's answer.

• Direct students to the example. Students tell you the exact words that Maria used (I think that there is too much violence on TV nowadays. I would ban some films ...).

• Students work in pairs and interview each other.

• Advise students to make a note of their partner's answers. Feedback.

Vocabulary 1 (page 86)

Phrasal verbs with *take*

Warm up: elicit from the students any phrasal verbs with *take* they know. Some they may know are:

take down (notes) = write down (notes)
take up (an offer) = accept (an offer)
take off (a plane takes off)
take to (someone) = start liking someone soon after you meet them
take over (something) = become responsible for, start being in charge of something
take after (someone) = resemble a member of your family, in appearance and/or behaviour
take (someone) *on* = employ, give someone a job

1

• Students read the sentences. Point out that the meaning of the phrasal verb they should use is in brackets at the end of each sentence. Explain that students must match the meaning with *take over, take on, take up* or *take to.*

• Students work in pairs and match each meaning to a phrasal verb. Feedback.

• Students complete the gaps with the phrasal verbs they have chosen. Students check their answers with the text on page 84. Feedback.

Answers

1	on	3	to
2	up	4	over

2

• Students complete the sentences with phrasal verbs with *take*. Point out the additional verbs in the box. Students check their answers in pairs. Feedback.

Answers

1	to	5	down
2	up	6	back
3	on	7	over
4	after		

Listening (page 87)

Warm up: explain to students that they are going to hear an extract from the latest Charles Pond movie, a humorous version of the famous Bond movies.

• As a fun activity do the following quick quiz with the students:

1 What is James Bond's favourite drink? (dry Martini, shaken not stirred)
2 What is Bond's code number? (007)
3 Is Bond's boss a man or a woman? (A man called 'M')
4 What is Bond's favourite sport? (Golf)
5 What does Bond like to eat? (caviar)
6 What kind of car does he drive? (A sports car – an Aston Martin)

1 🔊

• Students read the true/false questions and in pairs predict whether they are true or false.

• Students listen to the tape to check their answers. Feedback.

Answers

1 False (She is called Number 2)
2 False (He drinks tea)
3 True (He's out of prison)
4 False (The Sahara)

2 🔊

• Students read the report. Students work in pairs and try to complete the sentences before listening to the tape.

• Students listen to the tape to check their answers. Feedback.

Answers

1	had admired	6	wanted to take
2	to make	7	had tried
3	he had eaten	8	would send
4	did	9	made
5	was a threat		

Tapescript (exercises 1 and 2)

NUMBER 2: Ah! Come in, Pond. I've been waiting for you.

POND: 003 and a half at your service, Number 2. (question 1,1)

NUMBER 2: Let me introduce you to my new assistant, Mr Honeybunch.

POND: My name's Pond, Charles Pond.

HONEYBUNCH: I know, sir.

POND: I know you know, but I like saying it. Pleased to meet you.

HONEYBUNCH: I'm honoured, sir. I've heard a lot about you. I've admired you ever since I was at school. (question 2,1)

POND: Thank you. I'm flattered.

HONEYBUNCH: Can I have your autograph, sir?

NUMBER 2: Shut up, Honeybunch. Now. First things first. A drink, Pond?

POND: I'll have the usual.

NUMBER 2: Tea?

POND: As always. (question 1, 1) On the rocks.

NUMBER 2: Two sugar cubes as always. Milk?

POND: Just a drop.

NUMBER 2: 88.5 degrees?

POND: That's right.

NUMBER 2: You always drink your tea at a temperature of 88.5 degrees, don't you Pond?

POND: Yes. That's how my mother always made it.

NUMBER 2: Mr Honeybunch, make Pond a cup of tea, will you? (question 2, 2) 88.5 degrees.

HONEYBUNCH: Yes, boss.

NUMBER 2: Now, Pond, let's get down to business. It's about Dr Magniolini. He's out of prison. (question 1, 3)

POND: You mean the Magniolini who runs the pizzeria in Camden Town? Oh no! I had the worst pizza in my life there. (question 2, 3) We've got to stop him at all costs, Number 2! He must never be allowed to make another pizza! And his tea is a threat to public health. He's a dangerous man, Number 2.

NUMBER 2: I see you're well informed, as always, Pond.

POND: I always do my homework, Number 2. (question 2, 4) Anyway, how can I forget a villain like Dr Franco Magniolini, the crazy millionaire who tried to take over all the pizzerias in London.

NUMBER 2: Oh yes, of course. We stopped him just in time.

POND: Does that chef still work for him?

NUMBER 2: You mean Manuel?

POND: The very same. Manuel, the meanest chef in town. His pizza margarita is pure poison.

NUMBER 2: Look, Pond, we haven't got time to talk about pizzas now. This time the threat is even greater.

POND: You mean he's going to open a Greek taverna?

NUMBER 2: Even worse than that, Pond. What Magniolini has in mind this time is not only a threat to peace, it's a threat to civilization as we know it. I'll go further. Magniolini's new scheme is a threat to British culture. It's a deadly threat to the British way of life itself. (question 2, 5)

POND: You mean ... you mean ...

NUMBER 2: Yes, Pond.

POND: Tea!

NUMBER 2: That's right, Pond. This time Magniolini is aiming very high. He wants the tea. Total control.

POND: You mean he wants to take over the world's tea supply? (question 2, 6) To control it?

NUMBER 2: Precisely, Pond. He wants the British Isles under his thumb. With all the tea in the world under his control, there will be nothing we can do to stop him. He'll be able to do whatever he likes.

POND: The British public will never accept any threat to tea-time. Number 2, this is serious.

NUMBER 2: I know, Pond. That's why we're sending you to the Sahara (question 1, 4) on the first flight tomorrow morning.

POND: The Sahara? Oh no!

NUMBER 2: Yes, that's where Magniolini's got his secret headquarters. That's where he's storing and then destroying the world's tea supplies. What's the problem, Pond? You've gone pale.

POND: But Number 2, the Sahara is a desert.

NUMBER 2: Correct, Pond. You know your geography!

POND: But the golf in the Sahara is terrible! I tried to play a game there once. (question 2,7)

NUMBER 2: And what happened?

POND: I kept losing the ball.

NUMBER 2: Well Pond, don't worry. Next time we'll send you to Scotland. (question 2,8)

POND: Great – the golf is excellent there.

HONEYBUNCH: Your tea, sir.

POND: Thanks. Mmmm. Nice. You make a good cup of tea, Honeybunch. (question 2, 9)

HONEYBUNCH: Thank you, sir. Just doing my job, sir.

NUMBER 2: You see, Pond, this tea is worth fighting for.

POND: You bet ... mmmm ... delicious.

Grammar 2 (page 87)

Reported speech: other changes

Presentation: write these sentences from the tapescript on the board. Elicit from students who said each sentence. Students change the sentences into reported speech:

'Can I have your autograph, sir?' (Honeybunch asked Pond if he could have his autograph.)
'This time Magniolini is aiming very high.' (Number 2 said that that time Magniolini was aiming very high.)
'Next time we'll send you to Scotland.' (Number 2 said that next time they would send Pond to Scotland.)

• Focus on the changes in the modal verbs and the demonstrative *this/that*.

Grammar box
• Direct students to the grammar box on page 87. Students read it for a minute and then close their books.

• Elicit how many of the changes from direct to reported speech they can remember. Add cases where no change is required (would, could, should). Point out that when using a reporting verb in the present tense, the direct speech tends to remain the same:

I work for UNICEF. He says he works for UNICEF.

1

☆ Text note

• UNICEF stands for the United Nations Children's Fund.

• Students read the quotations from Roger Moore and in pairs rewrite them as reported speech. Tell them to refer to the grammar box for help. Feedback.

Answers
1 Moore said that those people lived in extreme poverty.
2 Moore said that with that money UNICEF could dramatically improve basic living conditions.
3 Moore told reporters that programmes would be set up to improve education for children there.
4 Moore told reporters that every seven seconds another child died, so he felt he should be a part of saving those children.
5 Moore said he was now an Ambassador for the UN Children's Fund and he hoped he would stay in that role.
6 Moore said they must/had to let people know in other countries that there were those who cared about them.
7 Moore told reporters/He said that his next job would be to get the Spice Girls working for UNICEF.

• Elicit from students other famous people who work for charities or social causes.

Vocabulary 2 (page 88)

Narrative styles

1

• Write the three headings (crime stories, ghost stories, journey stories) on the board.

• Students work in groups and brainstorm words associated with these stories. Feedback, writing students' ideas under the correct heading.

• Direct students to the words in the box. Make sure they understand them.

• Students complete the chart with the words in the box. Feedback.

Answers
Crime stories: commit, murder, catch (a thief), dangerous, charge (someone with a crime), violent, arrest (a suspect, criminal)
Ghost stories: haunted, creak (of a stair, door), dangerous (haunted house), mist (around the haunted house), spooky (atmosphere), fear (of ghosts, being alone in a haunted house), strange (events, happenings in haunted house).
Journey stories: check in, catch (a bus), set off (on a journey), dangerous (trip), mist (delayed take off), arrive (at your destination), suitcase (luggage), delay (take-off, departure)

2

• Students work in pairs to complete the sentences using words or phrases from exercise 1.

Answers
1	committed	6	mist
2	creaked	7	set off
3	dangerous	8	arrive
4	suitcase	9	spooky
5	check in	10	delayed

Writing (page 88)

Narrative composition

1

• Students read the instructions and the story to answer these gist questions. Emphasize that they should ignore the notes on the composition at this stage.

Where was Pond going? (Namumba)
Why did Pond's boss tell him to take a gun? (Because he would need it. Dr X meant business.)
Who left a message for Pond under his door? (Lola)
What was strange about the message? (Lola always spelt her name with two 'ls' not one.)

2

• Students read the story again. Focus on the notes and ask students to decide whether the story matches the notes. Students work in pairs. Feedback with reference to the story and the notes.

• Students rewrite the story to improve it. You could assign the story as homework.

• In the next lesson students exchange stories and compare them with the model on page 125 of the Student's Book. Students decide if they are better and why. Feedback.

3

• Students complete the sentences using the sequencing expressions given.

Answers

1 suddenly
2 As soon as, Then
3 After, About an hour later
4 Finally
5 First, The next day

4

• Students tick (✔) which of the expressions they think would be useful in their story.

Answers

Afterwards, He heard a strange sound, suddenly, to threaten someone, He fired his gun, It was freezing outside, then, that night, to blackmail someone, the snow was falling, darkness had fallen, 'Don't move or I'll shoot', He said he would…, dangerous, suspect something/someone of something

5

• Students work individually and choose one of the sentences in the box to end their story.

• Assign the story as homework. Remind students to use the paragraph plan and the expressions and grammar taught in this unit.

• If you think students need more guidance, they can brainstorm ideas for their story in pairs using the paragraph plan.

• In the next lesson students exchange and read stories making any necessary corrections and changes.

• Mark the stories and set a time limit in another lesson for feedback.

Sample composition (176 words)

There were no lights on anywhere in the old house, but I was sure I had heard a noise. I knocked on the door. 'Hello!' I shouted, but there was no answer. I knew that the house had been empty for a long time, so where had the noise come from? Then I noticed the door was open.

I had been into the house once before, when I was very young. A friend had lived here and I had often played in the garden. It was freezing cold, dark and spooky but moonlight shone in through a large window. I closed the front door and it creaked loudly.

I was in the living room. The furniture was covered in dust and there were cobwebs everywhere. There was a bookcase with a desk next to it. On the desk there was a book. As I walked toward it I saw that it was open.

Someone had underlined the words: I am alone and I remembered that I had seen this book before. Suddenly, I heard a noise behind me.

14 Art and artists

Topics
Picasso, Velazquez, my favourite photograph, Van Gogh

Grammar
Reported questions
Indirect questions

Vocabulary
Verb + preposition
Adjective + preposition

Reading
'A meeting with Picasso': multiple matching (headings)

Listening
Interview with a photographer: blank filling

Speaking
Describing a painting

Writing
Descriptive article (a painting)

Reading (pages 90–91)

☆ Text notes

• Pablo Ruiz Picasso (1881–1973) was born in Malaga, Spain. He was a painter, sculptor and ceramic worker. He lived part of his early life in Barcelona but most of his life was spent in Paris where his work went through various periods (blue, pink, Cubist, classical and surrealist were the most important periods in his artistic life) and made him one of the most well-known and richest painters of the twentieth century. He was influenced by African art, especially masks. His most famous painting is undoubtedly *Guernica* (1937), which condemns the horrors of war. It followed the Nazi bombing of a Basque village in northern Spain.

Warm up: if possible, have copies of paintings on show during these lessons (take magazines, posters or books of paintings to class). Try and have a copy of Picasso's *Guernica* in class during the reading comprehension. It would be a good idea to ask students to bring a favourite painting or photograph to class.

• Establish the topic of the text by sticking pictures of paintings around the room. Students work in pairs and discuss which is their favourite and why. Feedback quickly.

1

• Direct students to the painting on page 90. In pairs students describe what they see (a portrait of a young man).

• Students read the article quickly to see if the painting is mentioned. Advise students to underline any reference to paintings by Picasso. Feedback with reference to the text.

2

• Students read the headings A–G first. Check they understand them.

• Set a time limit. Students read the text again to match headings with paragraphs. Point out that there is an extra heading which they will not need to use. Feedback, with reference to the text.

Answers

1 E	4 C	
2 G	5 A	
3 D	6 B	F is not used

3

• Students read the definitions. In pairs, they try to think of an expression that matches each one without reading the text.

• Students read the text and check their answers. Advise them to underline the part of the text where they found the expression. Feedback with reference to the text.

Grammar 1 (page 91)

Reported questions

Presentation: write these sentences on the board:
She asked me where did I live?
He wanted to know if had I been to the cinema?

• Elicit from students what is wrong with them. (Word order and structure should be the same as for statements, not interrogative.)

• Students correct them. (She asked me where I lived. He wanted to know if I had been to the cinema.)

Grammar box
• Direct students to the grammar box on page 91. Check students understand by asking these check questions:
What do you notice about the word order of reported questions? (It is the same as for statements.)
What happens to question words like who, which, what in reported questions? (They are repeated from the direct question.)
Which words do we use in reporting yes/no questions? (If or whether)

1

• Students rewrite the direct questions as reported questions. Point out that they can use the grammar box to help them.

Answers

1 The teacher asked her if she liked Picasso's work.
2 She wanted to know where Picasso was from.
3 She wanted to know why I didn't take up painting as a hobby.
4 He asked me if/whether I had ever painted a picture.

Optional activity

• Use some of the questions from exercise 1 to initiate a class discussion.

Do you like Picasso's work?
Why don't you take up painting as a hobby?
Have you ever painted a picture?

2

• Direct students to the photograph on page 91. Elicit that the man in the photograph is Picasso. Explain that students are going to read a report of an interview with Picasso.

• Students read the text quickly to answer these gist questions:
What clothes are mentioned? (a sailor shirt)
What insect is mentioned? (a butterfly)
What jobs are mentioned? (sailor, writer, businessman, painter)

• Students work in pairs to complete the text. Point out that some of the words can be used more than once. Feedback.

Answers

1	whether	7	wanted
2	wore	8	was
3	was	9	written
4	whether	10	did
5	didn't	11	was
6	could	12	wrote

Speaking (page 92)

☆ Text notes

• The painting is *Las Meninas* or *The Family of Philip IV* (1656) by Velázquez and is one of the most famous paintings in the world. *Meninas* was the name given to the noble young maids in the Spanish court. In this painting they are the two girls on the left and right of the young princess. The king and the queen are at the front of the picture but we only see their reflection in the mirror at the back.

Las Meninas is also a self-portrait of the painter and we see him at work on the left.

In the centre of the picture is the five-year-old princess refusing to accept what the *menina* is offering her to drink.

In the bottom right hand corner are two people, a woman and a boy who is putting his foot on a dog.

There is a mysterious figure in the background, about to leave the room. Who could he be?

• Diego Rodriguez Velázquez (1599–1660) was a Spanish painter. His patron was King Philip IV. He painted many portraits of the royal family and members of the court. He had a huge influence on the Impressionists and on Picasso.

1

• Direct students to the picture on page 92. Ask them to identify these people:
the painter, the princess, the maids, the king and queen.

• Students work in pairs to answer the questions. Feedback with reference to the picture.

Answers

1 On the left of the picture, holding a paintbrush
2 a dog, two people, maids trying to give the princess a drink
3 a man walking up the stairs

2

• Students read the statements and questions. Make sure they understand them. Students discuss in pairs who might be thinking each one. Feedback, encouraging students to give reasons for their answers.

Answers

1 This must the maid on the left – the one kneeling down – offering the princess a drink. It might be medicine.
2 This must be the boy in the bottom right hand corner who is putting his foot on the dog.
3 This must be the painter. He is thinking about the portrait he is painting and wondering how much he is going to get paid for it. He believes the painting is a very good one.
4 This could be the dog wishing the little boy would stop bothering him.
5 This must be the princess refusing to have her drink/medicine.
6 This could be the man in the background who is about to leave the room. The man could be courtier or a guard and he is looking back at the princess and the painter and the servants and wondering what they are all doing.

3

• Students work in pairs and choose one or two people in the painting to interview. Explain that they will have to take it in turns to be these people and answer the questions.

• Give students time to write their questions. Direct them to the examples for ideas. Feedback, writing some of the questions on the board.

• Students interview each other. Advise them to make a note of their partner's answers. Feeding back could be very amusing. Students feedback using reported speech, telling the class what their partner said.

Vocabulary 1 (page 92)

Verb + preposition

Warm up: write these verbs on the board:
listen
talk

• Elicit from students the prepositions that follow these verbs (*to, about*).

• Elicit from students any other verbs they know that take these or other prepositions.

1

• Students read the sentences and correct the mistakes.

Answers

1 I'm listening to some music.
2 We talked about the problem of drugs.
3 Every Saturday evening I go to a cafeteria.
4 I can't stop thinking about you!
5 I arrived in London at about ten o'clock.

2

• Students complete the questions using the correct prepositions. Feedback.

Answers

1	to	4	in
2	to	5	on
3	about	6	in

Listening (page 93)

1 📼

• Direct students to the photograph on page 93. Students work in pairs and describe what they can see. Feedback quickly.

• Students answer the questions in pairs. Feedback, encouraging students to give reasons for their answers.

Suggested answers

1 It must have been taken in the back of a car on a hot summer's day.
2 They are probably brothers.
3 He or she may have taken it because the boys look very peaceful/the colours are nice/it was a holiday.

• Students listen to the interview and check their answers. Feedback.

Answers

1 In the car, which had stopped at a bridge.
2 They are twin brothers. They're very close.
3 He took it to show the close contact between the boys.

2 📼

• Students read the notes. In pairs students try and complete the notes before listening to the interview again.

• Students listen again to check their answers. Feedback.

Answers

1 in the third class of High School
2 have a go
3 old buildings
4 people
5 close
6 chatting to
7 holiday
8 two little angels

3

• Explain to students that the twins in this photo are the same boys as on page 13 in picture 6. Students look back at page 13 and, in pairs, compare the photos. Feedback.

Suggested answers

In the picture on page 93 they are almost babies, they are still and peaceful; they are lying down.
In the picture on page 13 the boys, now teenagers, are active, energetic, jumping high in the air. In the early picture they are in harmony and in the later picture they are in competition.

Tapescript (exercises 1 and 2)

INTERVIEWER: When did you take up photography? I mean, you started out as a painter, didn't you? What made you decide to concentrate on photographs?

BUKOVSKY: I think it was because I found it easier to say what I wanted to say – to express myself – through photography. I don't know whether I've managed it, but that's what I was trying to do.

INTERVIEWER: How old were you when you took up photography? When did you take your first photograph?

BUKOVSKY: How old was I?

INTERVIEWER: Yes, when did you take your first photo?

BUKOVSKY: Well, I must have been in the third class of High School. **(question 2,1)**

INTERVIEWER: What was it that made you interested in photography? Did your parents buy you a camera as a present or what?

BUKOVSKY: Well, there was a camera in the house and my mother said I could have it. She told me to have a go at taking pictures, so I did. **(question 2,2)**

INTERVIEWER: And what kind of pictures did you take in those days? What were your first attempts?

BUKOVSKY: My first attempts were pictures of buildings, old buildings – you know, buildings that were in ruins and would soon disappear altogether. **(question 2, 3)**

INTERVIEWER: And what was your mother's reaction when she saw your first pictures?

BUKOVSKY: She wondered why I didn't take pictures of people. **(question 2, 4)** So then I started taking pictures of people and I'm still working on that.

INTERVIEWER: Do you mean portraits?

BUKOVSKY: Well, partly, but I'm interested in human activity, human life in general. Their behaviour. If you can capture it. That's what interests me more than anything else. This picture of the two boys expresses something important in their relationship. They're very close. **(question 2, 5)**

INTERVIEWER: Why did you take this picture? Were you trying to express something specific?

BUKOVSKY: The basic thing was to show the close contact between them. **(question 1, 3)**

INTERVIEWER: How do you go about taking pictures of people? What do you do exactly?

BUKOVSKY: Well, you can't just go up to them and start taking pictures. You approach them and you start chatting to them. **(question 2, 6)** I don't just bring the camera out and click.

INTERVIEWER: What about this one – the two boys?

BUKOVSKY: Well, as you can see, they're twins. **(question 1,2)** Anyway, we were on holiday with some friends at the time, **(question 2, 7)** and we'd stopped at a bridge for a rest; **(question 1, 2)** Our two boys were very tired and I saw them lying there looking like two little angels; **(question 2, 8)** I liked the way the sunlight was coming through the windows – it made everything look so peaceful. It seemed to me a perfect picture of peace and harmony.

Grammar 2 (page 93)

Indirect questions

Presentation: write these incorrect sentences on the board:
Have you any idea what means 'Meninas'? (Have you any idea what *Meninas* means?)
Do you know where is the nearest chemist? (Do you know where the nearest chemist is?)

• Elicit from students what is wrong with them. Students correct them.

• Elicit from students what type of questions they are (indirect).

Grammar box
• Direct students to the grammar box on page 93. Make sure students understand by asking these check questions:
How do we begin indirect questions?
Does the word order change in indirect questions?
Do tenses change in indirect questions?

1

• Students rewrite the direct questions as indirect questions. Feedback.

Answers

1 Have you any idea where Lima is?
2 Would you mind telling me who that woman over there is?
3 Can you tell me what time the film starts?
4 Could you tell me where the nearest bank is?
5 Do you know what time it is?

2

• Students skim through the dialogue before they start to complete it to answer these gist questions:
Where is Edessa? (near Thessaloniki)
What jobs do the speaker's parents do? (a teacher and a lawyer)
What does the speaker want to do? (become a nurse)

• Students complete the dialogue with indirect questions. Feedback.

Answers

1 you come from
2 that is?
3 your parents do?
4 you want to do/you're going to do?
5 you want to become a nurse?

Vocabulary 2 (page 94)

Adjective + preposition

Warm up: write these adjectives on the board:
keen, good, famous, bored, tired, pleased, proud, interested, angry, sorry

• Elicit from students which preposition follows each one. Feedback.

Answers

keen on, good at, famous for, bored with, tired of, pleased with/about, proud of, interested in, angry with/about, sorry about/for

• Students read the text quickly to answer these gist questions:
Where was Alicia born? (Italy)
What does she want to study? (art)
What isn't she good at? (music)
Where is she going to live? (US, in New Orleans)

• Students choose the correct prepositions. Feedback.

Answers

1	in	6	at
2	about	7	of
3	on	8	for
4	of	9	of
5	about		

Writing (page 94)

Descriptive article

1

• Direct students to the photographs on page 94. Students work in pairs and describe what they can see. Feedback.

Answers

1 a man and woman embracing.
2 a country scene. There's a house in the background and a river. There are some people and a horse in a boat on the left of the picture.
3 a piece of modern art. There are squares, circles, colours and writing.

• Students discuss which pictures they like and do not like. Feedback, encouraging students to explain what they like/dislike about them.

• You may want to write some useful language for describing pictures on the board to help them with this first exercise:
in the background/foreground
in the middle of
in the top right/left hand corner
in the bottom right/left hand corner
on the left/right
at the top/bottom
landscape
portrait
still life
interesting, unusual, strange, abstract, realistic, everyday, dark, gloomy, cheerful

2

☆ Text notes

• Vincent Van Gogh (1853–1890) was a Dutch Post-Impressionist painter. His early work showed Dutch peasant life in dark, sombre colours. In 1886 he went to live in France. He began to use pure, bright colours. Some of his paintings began to show the fear of madness and death. Indeed, his last years were spent in asylums. In the end, he shot himself.

• Direct students to the painting on page 95. Ask the students if they recognize the painting and who it was painted by.

• Students read the instructions and the text about Van Gogh and answer the questions. Feedback briefly.

Answers

1 Van Gogh was born in Holland.
2 The painting is called *Bedroom at Arles*.
3 The original is in the Riksmuseum in Amsterdam.

3

• Students read the text again and complete it using the appropriate cohesive items. Point out that same words can be used more than once. Students check their answers in pairs. Feedback.

Answers

1	This	6	the/this
2	it	7	it
3	this	8	my
4	his	9	the/this
5	He	10	the

4

• Students read headings A–D. Make sure they understand them.

• Students read the text again and match headings with paragraphs. Feedback.

Answers

1 D Introduction
2 A Background information
3 C Why I like this picture
4 B Summing up

5

• Students read the list of types of language.

• Students work in pairs and give one example of each type of language. Feedback.

• Students find and underline examples in the text. Students compare their answers in pairs. Feedback.

Answers

1 **Indirect speech:** Van Gogh replied that he wanted the colours to make everything look happier, he added that the painting should make us feel relaxed
2 **Passive voice:** the painting is called, it was painted
3 **Past continuous:** Van Gogh was living
4 **Cause and effect:** as a result
5 **Time expressions:** At the time, Today

6

• Students read the instructions for the writing exercise. Assign the article as homework. Remind students to use the expressions and grammar used in this unit, the model on page 95 and the paragraph plan.

• When students bring in their article, it would be nice if they could bring a copy of the painting or photo it is about, too.

• In the next lesson students exchange and read articles making corrections or changes if necessary.

• Mark the articles and set a time limit in another lesson for feedback.

Sample article (180 words)

One of my favourite paintings is 'The Dance Class' by Degas. Degas was famous for painting ballet dancers and this is one of his most well-known works. It was painted in about 1900.

The painting shows a class of ballet students listening to the teacher. They are in the dance class which is a large room with a shiny wooden floor. In the foreground and background, we can see a group of young dancers - some of them are sitting on the floor, others are standing. Most of them are paying attention to what the teacher is saying. The teacher, who is an elderly man, is standing almost in the middle of the picture, leaning on a stick.

I like it because the colours are bright and warm. I particularly like the green walls which go with the green ribbons some of the girls are wearing. The yellow dresses and bright red make me feel happy and optimistic.

Degas was an impressionist painter and sculptor. Many of his paintings are now in the Louvre in Paris. He died in 1917.

15 Our wonderful world

Topics
The Monarch butterfly, the zoo, animals, the circus, safari holidays

Grammar
Time clauses
Gerunds and infinitives

Vocabulary
Noun + preposition
Animals

Reading
'Monarch without a kingdom': gapped text

Listening
Four speakers talking about animals: multiple matching

Speaking
Pairwork task (planning a trip to the zoo): Information gap (eagles quiz)

Writing
Transactional letter (asking for information about a holiday)

Reading (pages 96–97)

☆ Text notes

• The Monarch Butterfly is a beautiful insect found in parts of North and South America. It is orange and black. For various reasons, explained in the text, it is in danger of extinction. The Monarch Butterfly travels enormous distances from North to Central America and back again and on the way encounters threats not only from nature but man-made threats such as pesticides and genetically modified crops.

• Maize is a tall American cereal plant. It is a source of oil and corn flour.

• Genetically Modified (GM) plants are designed to produce large quantities of particular varieties of food crops. There are indications that the genetic interference is harmful to health.

• Greenpeace is an international, independent organization whose aim is to protect the environment. It is well-known for its occasionally spectacular protests against threats to the environment.

Warm up: elicit from students what *monarch* means (a king or queen) and what a *kingdom* is (the land controlled by a king or queen).

• Write the title *Monarch without a kingdom* on the board and ask students to predict what the text is going to be about.

• Students read the text quickly to check their predictions.

• Write these numbers on the board. Tell students they all refer in some way to the Monarch Butterfly (shown in the photographs). Students work in pairs to guess what they might refer to:

3 (length of butterfly's body)
1 (what it weighs in grammes)
5,000 (kilometres it travels each year)
70 (percentage that die en route to Mexico)
48 (number of hours it takes for GM maize to kill a butterfly)
100 (species of butterfly in danger of extinction)

• Students read the text and scan for the information. Feedback.

I

• Students read the text again and answer the questions. Advise them to underline the part of the text where they find the answers. Feedback, with reference to the text.

> #### Answers
> 1 The US (line 10) and Mexico (line 2/11)
> 2 5,000 km (line 6)
> 3 Strong winds, rain, snowstorms (line 18); genetically modified maize (lines 29–30)
> 4 November (lines 12) winter (line 19) April (line 24)
> 5 scientific progress (line 27) genetically modified maize (line 30)

2

• Point out the numbers 1–5 in the text. Explain that these numbers mark the position of missing sentences.

• Students read sentences A–E carefully and underline key words which will help them to put the sentences back into the correct place in the text.

• Students work alone or in pairs. They read each paragraph carefully, focusing on the space where a sentence is missing. Point out that they should read what comes before and after the space to find connections with the missing sentences. Feedback, eliciting which words helped students decide where the sentences go.

Answers

1	A	4	B
2	C	5	D
3	E		

3

• Students read the definitions and in pairs try and guess the words before they read the text again.

• Students check their answers with the text. Advise them to underline the part of the text where they find the word. Feedback with reference to the text.

Answers

1 extinction (line 4)
2 survive (line 8)
3 reaches (line 11)
4 flapping (line 15)
5 beginning (line 24)
6 calendar (line 25)
7 experiments (line 29)

Grammar 1 (page 97)

Time clauses

Presentation: students brainstorm the time expressions they already know.

Grammar box
Direct students to the grammar box on page 97. Make sure students understand the example.

• In pairs, students make example sentences using the other time expressions. Feedback, writing a few examples on the board.

1

• Students complete the sentences and check their answers with the text.

Answers

1 reaches (line 11)
2 get (line 23)

2

• Students complete the sentences using the verbs given. Students check their answers in pairs. Feedback.

Answers

1	flies	4	rains
2	am	5	fetch
3	arrives	6	gives

3

• Students choose the correct time expression. Feedback, encouraging students to give reasons for their choices.

Answers

1	As soon as	5	when
2	before	6	until
3	By	7	Once
4	After		

Speaking (page 98)

1

• Use the pictures on page 98 to introduce the topic of zoos. Students work in pairs and describe what they see. Feedback briefly.

• Students read the instructions. Make sure they understand them.

• Students work with a partner, discuss the pictures and decide how they are going to spend the time. Point out the box of expressions under the pictures.

• Feedback, encouraging students to use the expressions in the box and to tell the class what they have decided. They can say whether they agreed or disagreed with their partner.

2

• Direct students to the photograph on page 98 and elicit from students if they know what kind of bird it is (an eagle). Ask if they know anything about eagles.

• Check that students understand this essential vocabulary:
wings, feathers, eyelids, nest
dive (to drop into water or through the air)
a ton (907.2 kilos in the US/1016 kilos in Britain)

• Explain that students are going to work in pairs to ask and answer questions about eagles. Student A will ask the questions on page 104 and student B will ask the questions on page 113. The answers to their partner's questions are also on the page.

• Point out that students should not confirm answers until they have both finished asking and answering questions. They can then give each other the answers.

• Feedback by asking a few random questions from the quiz and checking the answers.

Vocabulary 1 (page 98)

Noun + preposition

Warm up: write these nouns on the board and elicit from students which preposition they are followed by:

respect (for)
recording (of)
book (about)

• Elicit examples.

1

• Students match the nouns in list A with the prepositions in list B.

Answers

1	b	5	g
2	d	6	f
3	a	7	c
4	e		

• Check that students understand the nouns by eliciting examples for each one.

2

• Students cover the noun and preposition combinations in exercise 1 and complete the sentences.

• Students check their answers by referring to exercise 1.

Answers

1	description	5	in
2	on	6	for
3	on	7	information
4	reply		

Listening (page 99)

Warm up: students identify the animals in the photographs. Ask if any of these animals can be found in their country. Ask if any are in danger of extinction.

• Check understanding of the following key words: *creatures* (animals), *habitat* (where animals live), *permit* (written permission to do something), *rod* (as in *fishing rod* for catching fish), *bait* (food, for example worms, you use to catch fish with).

1

• Students listen and say which animal each of the four speakers is talking about. Feedback.

Answers

1	the jaguar	3	the bear
2	fish (salmon)	4	the eagle

2

• Explain to students that they are going to listen to the speakers again, but this time they will have to focus on details.

• Students read questions A–E. Make sure they understand them.

• Students underline the key words in each question that will help them find the information.

• Students listen again and match the speakers with the questions. Feedback, with specific reference to what the speakers said.

Answers

A   2 (Every Sunday morning; it's really fun; I enjoy catching fish)
B   1 (I realized I'd forgotten to put a film in my camera.)
C   4 (Thank you all for coming; and when we're all ready, I'll begin. Today, I'm going to talk to you about)
D   3 (illegal hunting)

Optional activity

• Write these sentences from the listening text on the board and ask students to complete them. This will help reinforce the grammar of time clauses dealt with earlier in the unit and introduce the new grammar points on gerund and infinitive.

1 As soon as the bear _____ *(appear).*
2 I love _____ *(watch)* them.
3 When I _____ *(get)* to sleep tonight, I'll dream of bears.
4 I love _____ *(go)* fishing.
5 There are some places where they don't let you _____ *(fish).*
6 I enjoy_____ *(catch)* fish.

Tapescript (exercises 1 and 2)

SPEAKER 1

We waited and waited for hours. Suddenly, I saw her: she was huge and she looked really beautiful. And wild, completely wild. She was just sixty metres away, with nothing between us but white sand. This <u>fantastic cat</u> **(question 1, c)** was walking straight towards me. I wasn't afraid – I just felt very angry with myself, because <u>I realized I'd forgotten to put a film in my camera</u>! **(question 2, B)** Thirty metres in front of me the jaguar stopped and stared for one long minute, before turning round and walking calmly back into the forest. I kept coming back to the same spot for three months, but I never saw her again.

SPEAKER 2

<u>Every Sunday morning</u> **(question 2, A)** I go to the river not far from here where there are <u>lots of fish</u>. **(question 1, d)** You've got to be careful where you go because there are some places they don't let you fish, and you need to have a special permit. I take a net and a fishing rod with me and some bait – you know, little worms that move about and get the attention of the fish. They love them. It really attracts them. I think <u>it's</u>

---

really fun. **(question 2, A)** It's nice and quiet, and I usually manage to catch at least two or three fish. I enjoy catching fish, **(question 2, A)** but I always throw them back in again before I go home.

SPEAKER 3

You see, the number of these creatures has been decreasing because its habitats – the areas where it lives, that is – have been destroyed. Illegal hunting **(question 2, D)** has also done it a lot of damage. Well I'm here today as a member of the Save the Wild Bear Fund, **(question 1, a)** and I'm going to take photos of it. I have to wait until one of them appears. Sometimes we wait until just before the sun comes up, when the bear **(question1, a)** usually comes down the mountain to find food. As soon as a bear appears, I'll be ready with my camera. I love watching them and really hope that my work will help to save them.

SPEAKER 4

Well, thank you all for coming, and when we're all ready, I'll begin. Right. Today, I'm going to talk to you **(question 2, C)** about the eagle **(question 1, b)** – well, a number of eagles, really. There are many different varieties, but the ones I'm going to talk about today have one thing in common: they are threatened with extinction. Let me begin with the Spanish Imperial Eagle. There are probably only a hundred or so of these large eagles now living in Spain. Most of them were actually living in Donana National Park, but there was an ecological disaster there a few years ago, which destroyed not only the park but the habitat of the Imperial Eagle, too.

Grammar 2 (page 99)

Infinitives and gerunds

Presentation: write these sentences on the board and elicit the mistakes:

I want going to the beach.
I keep to forget my glasses.

Grammar box

• Direct students to the grammar box on page 99.

• Students read the grammar box and in pairs add more examples to each column. Feedback.

• Point out that some verbs can be followed by either the infinitive or gerund but with a change of meaning. For example:
She stopped talking to her friend. (They had had a quarrel, perhaps.)
She stopped to talk to her friend. (As she met her walking along the street, she stopped in order to speak to her.)

1

• Students work in pairs and add the expressions to the appropriate column.

Answers

Infinitive with *to*	Infinitive without *to*	Gerund
want	you'd better	deny
refuse	can	suggest
manage	will	enjoy
prefer	should	keep

2

• Students complete the sentences.

• Point out that some of the verbs have been referred to in exercise 1, others they will have to try and guess. Students check their answers in pairs. Feedback.

Answers

1	going	4	lying
2	to go	5	seeing
3	visit	6	to ask

3

• Students read the text to answer these gist questions:
Does the writer enjoy going to the zoo? (No)
Where does the writer prefer to go? (the cinema)

• Students complete the text, with the appropriate form of the verb in brackets. Feedback.

Answers

1	to go	5	do
2	looking	6	to persuade
3	to see/seeing	7	going
4	seeing	8	to convince

Vocabulary 2 (page 100)

Animals

Warm up: write these headings on the board:
Wild animals *Insects*
Sea creatures *Birds*

• Elicit from students examples of each group and write them under the correct heading. For example:
Wild animals: *tiger, lion*
Insects: *wasp, bee, ant*
Sea creatures: *seal, dolphin*
Birds: *swallow, sparrow*

1

• Students read the words in the box. Make sure they know what each one is by asking the following check questions:
Which animal is very big and has a trunk? (elephant)
Which animal lives in the forest and likes honey? (bear)
Which insect makes a buzzing sound and makes honey? (bee)

Which bird is called the king of the birds? (eagle)
Which animal has one or two humps on its back? (camel)
Which animal is like a big cat with stripes? (tiger)
Which insect has a reputation for good organization and for hard work? (ant)
Which is the biggest creature in the sea? (whale)

• Students add the words in the box to the correct column.

Answers

Wild animals	Insects	Sea creatures	Birds
elephant	bee	seal	swallow
bear	butterfly	shark	dove
camel	ant	dolphin	eagle
snake	mosquito	whale	hawk
lion	fly	falcon	
tiger	spider		
monkey	cockroach		
leopard			
zebra			
giraffe			

2

• Students read the descriptions and match each one with an animal from exercise 1. Feedback by asking which key words in the description helped students to make their choice.

Answers

1	lion	4	bee
2	camel	5	monkeys
3	snake		

Optional activity

• As a fun activity do an animal quiz with the students:
It is the tallest animal. (giraffe)
It looks like a small eagle and it eats small animals. (hawk)
This bird has been a symbol of peace since Noah's Ark. (dove)
This insect spins a web and has eight legs. (spider)
This is a very small insect, almost invisible, which stings. (mosquito)

• Students could make up their own definitions and add to the quiz.

Writing (pages 100–101)

Transactional letter

☆ Text notes

• Namibia is a country in southwest Africa. It has borders with Angola, Zambia, Botswana, and South Africa. The capital is Windhoek.

• The Maldives are a group of small islands forming an independent country in the Indian Ocean, Southwest of Sri Lanka. The capital is Male.

Warm up: direct students to the advertisements on pages 100 and 101. Students look at the photos and describe what they see. Elicit *safari* and *cruise*. Make sure students know what these are by asking the following check questions:
Which holiday is on the water? (cruise)
Which involves wild animals? (safari)

1

• Students look more carefully at the two holidays and discuss in pairs which one they would prefer to go on. Feedback encouraging students to give reasons for their answers.

2

• Direct students to the model letter on page 101. Students read the letter quickly to answer these gist questions:
When does she want to go on holiday? (July)
What do they like doing? (walking, riding)
What information does she want about animals? (which ones live in the park)
Where does she want to fly from? (Paris)

• Students read the letter again. In pairs they find and underline the sentences that do not belong. Feedback. Elicit from students which famous song they are from ('Wonderful World', Louis Armstrong).

Answers

I see skies of blue. (4)
And I think to myself. (2)
I see friends shaking hands. (6)
I see trees of green. (1)
I hear babies cry (9)
The colours of the rainbow. (5)
What a wonderful world. (3)
…they're really saying. (7)
I love you. (8)

3

• Students write the sentences from the song in their notebooks. In pairs they try to decide which order they go in.

• Students listen to the song to check their answers (see answers above).

4 ▣

• Students brainstorm in groups as many words or lines from the song as they know or remember. Feedback, writing their ideas on the board.

• Students listen to the song again and write it down line by line.

What a Wonderful World

I see trees of green, red roses too
I see them bloom for me and you
And I think to myself, what a wonderful world

I see skies of blue and clouds of white
The bright blessed day, the dark sacred night
And I think to myself, what a wonderful world

The colours of the rainbow, so pretty in the sky
Are also on the faces of people going by
I see friends shaking hands, saying 'How do
    you do?'
They're really saying 'I love you'

I hear babies crying, I watch them grow
They'll learn much more than I'll ever know
Yes, I think to myself, what a wonderful world,
And I think to myself, what a wonderful world

5

• Students read the instructions. Make sure they understand them.

• Assign the letter for homework. In the next lesson students exchange and read letters making corrections and changes if necessary.

• Mark the letters and set a time limit in another lesson for feedback.

Sample letter (131 words)

Dear Sir or Madam,

I am writing to ask for more information about the Ocean safari holiday which I saw advertised in the newspaper. Firstly, I would like to ask if I'll get the opportunity to stop at any of the islands. I am very keen to see some of them. I am also interested in water sports and would like to know if we have to pay extra for those.

I would also like to know how many crew members will be on the boat.

Could you please send me more information about these things and also about the cost of the holiday. In your advertisement you refer to double and twin accommodation. Does this mean single people will have to share a room?

I look forward to hearing from you.

Yours faithfully,

Revision (Units 13-15)

Answers

1
1. B
2. D
3. B
4. B
5. D
6. B
7. C
8. D
9. A
10. C
11. A
12. B
13. A
14. D
15. B

2
1. it
2. on
3. make
4. let
5. at
6. go
7. using/taking
8. as
9. to
10. at
11. get
12. next
13. soon
14. in
15. leave

3
1. avoid spilling
2. don't mind waiting
3. would rather read
4. made the students stay
5. let us leave
6. told us he had found
7. had been sipping
8. her why she liked
9. him how he felt
10. asked him which

4
1. it
2. ✓
3. to
4. ✓
5. has
6. them
7. the
8. ✓
9. for
10. ✓
11. to
12. ✓
13. most
14. ✓
15. which

5
1. relaxation
2. extinction
3. organizations
4. information
5. accommodation
6. expensive
7. equipment
8. comfortable

Extra writing activities

Writing

Letter of complaint
(Units 3, 15)

1 You went on a one-week package holiday to Britain. You were very disappointed with the holiday. Read the Cosmos Tours advertisement and the notes you made about the holiday.

2 Tick (✔) the information you think you should include in your letter of complaint to Cosmos Tours.

1 your reason for writing
2 the dates of the holiday
3 which members of your family were on the tour
4 what was wrong with the visits
5 your hobbies and interests
6 what was wrong with the travel
7 your profession
8 what was wrong with the accommodation

3 Choose the most appropriate expressions for your formal letter of complaint.

1 a Dear Sir or Madam,
  b Dear John and Mary,
2 a I am writing to ask for information about ...
  b I am writing to complain about ...
3 a Firstly I would like to complain about ...
  b Let's begin with ...
4 a Let's look at the hotel
  b As for the accommodation ...
5 a You kept us hanging around at the airport ...
  b We were kept waiting at the airport ...
6 a In your ad ...
  b In your advertisement ...
7 a We'd like you to give us our money back ...
  b We would be grateful if you would return our money ...

See Britain with Cosmos Tours! Visit the great city of London with its museums and palaces.

Visit Warwick with its fine castle, See Stratford, birthplace of Shakespeare and many, many more unforgettable places!

• Quick and easy travel by air and by coach.
• Visits arranged by us – you don't have to worry about anything.
• Accommodation in quiet four-star hotels

Relax and enjoy your Cosmos Tour!

We did the British museum in one hour!

We saw Buckingham Palace from the outside only!

We paid extra for visits to Warwick and Stratford!

Coach delayed

Hotel in London noisy and food awful

Ask for money back

4 Write your letter of complaint to Cosmos Tours. Read the advertisment carefully and use the notes, the formal expressions in exercise 3 and the plan below to help you. Write between 120 and 180 words.

Paragraph 1: Say who you are and why you are writing.
Paragraph 2: Say why you were not happy about the holiday.
Paragraph 3: Say what was wrong with the visit to London. Say why you were unhappy about the visits to Warwick and Stratford. Say what was wrong with the hotel in London and the travel arrangements.
Paragraph 4: Conclude your letter by expressing your disappointment and asking for your money back.
Sign off: Yours faithfully,

Letter of application (Unit 1)

1 You have seen an advertisement in *Student News* for summer jobs for students. Read the advert and your notes.

Paradise Hotel
Summer jobs
for students

- Smart part-time waiters/ waitresses required at seaside hotel
- Knowledge of English required as well as a friendly personality
- If you are hard-working and efficient and are free this summer, write to us now!

(Applicants with previous experience preferred.)

smart appearance

English: FCE (Grade A)

friendly and patient

good student

free July-mid August

Can send reference

Have worked in my parents' supermarket

2 Complete this letter using the phrases below.

1 I can communicate well ...
2 I also have some experience
3 Firstly ...
4 I also believe ...
5 I am writing to apply
6 Finally, ...
7 I like ...
8 I would like to add ...
9 As for my personal qualities ...
10 As a student ...
11 I am very keen to ...
12 I believe I am ...
13 I think this will be useful ...

Dear Sir or Madam,

(1) _____ for the job of waiter in your hotel advertised in *Student News*. (2) _____ a suitable person for the job for the following reasons. (3) _____ I have already passed the English First Certificate (Grade A) and (4) _____ practise my English further. I had an opportunity to use my English on holiday last year and I believe (5) _____ language. (6) _____ in the parents' supermarket and (7) _____ of serving customers in my advertised. (8) _____ for the job hard-working. (9) _____ I think I am friendly and making new friends. (10) _____ meeting people and marks in most of my subjects. (11) _____ I get good quite patient and polite. (12) _____ I am I have a smart appearance. _____ that I think (13) _____ I will be free from the beginning of July to the middle of August.

I look forward to hearing from you.

3 Write a letter of application expressing your interest in the job. Read the advertisement carefully and use the notes, the expressions in exercise 2 and the plan below to help you. Write between 120 and 180 words.

Paragraph 1: Why you are writing
Paragraph 2: Language and experience
Paragraph 3: Personal qualities, appearance
Paragraph 4: Availability and closing
Sign off: Yours faithfully,

Photocopiable

Writing

Informal letter (Unit 2)

1 You have received a postcard from an old friend of yours who went to live in England two years ago. Read the postcard and decide what you are going to write in your reply.

Dear ...,

Hi. ..... It's been ages since I heard from you. How are things? I'm just writing to say I might be coming to Greece in August and wondered whether you're having a party again on your birthday like you did last year.

By the way, I got great marks in my exams.

Write soon, because I have to make plans.

Take care,

John

2 Look at expressions 1–12. Choose the most appropriate expressions for an informal letter.

1 a Dear Mr Jones,
  b Dear John,
2 a It was great to hear from you the other day.
  b Many thanks for your recent letter.
3 a I apologize for not writing for such a long time
  b Sorry I haven't written for so long ...
4 a The fact is, I've been in bed with flu.
  b I would like to inform you that I have been ill with influenza.
5 a I'm glad things are going well at school.
  b I was pleased to hear that your school work has been satisfactory.

6 a I would like to invite you to attend my birthday party.
  b Anyway, I'm also writing to ask you if you can come to my birthday party.
7 a It'll be on August 8 (as always!)
  b The party, of course, will be held on August 8.
8 a I've also asked a lot of friends from camp last year.
  b I have invited several friends from camp last year.
9 a It'd be great if you could come.
  b I would be pleased if you could come.
10 a By the way, if you want to stay a few days
  b Moreover, if you wish to stay a few days
11 a That's all for now.
  b In conclusion ...
12 a I look forward to hearing from you,
  b Write soon,

3 Write a letter to your friend, explaining why you have not written for such a long time and inviting him to your birthday party. Read the postcard carefully and use the informal expressions from exercise 2 and the plan below to help you. Write between 120 and 180 words.

Paragraph 1: Refer to your friend's postcard. Apologize for not writing and explain why.

Paragraph 2: Invite your friend to the party. Explain where and when it will be.

Paragraph 3: Mention other people you have invited. Say why everyone will have a good time.

Paragraph 4: Say how much you want your friend to come. Invite your friend to stay a few days. Close the letter.

Sign off: (Keep it friendly)

Photocopiable

110

©Macmillan Publishers Limited 2001. This sheet may be photocopied for use in class.

Writing

Short story (Units 4, 9, 13)

1 Match these sentences with the correct pictures.

1 They drove at top speed through the centre of London. ____

2 One day last week, Alice was sitting in the café of a London bus station, waiting for a coach home. ____

3 Alice saw the woman driving off in a taxi. ____

4 Alice opened the bag and was surprised to find someone else's passport and documents. ____

5 Suddenly, the woman got up, taking Alice's bag with her by mistake. ____

6 Just when Alice was ready to give up, she saw a woman getting into her car. ____

2 Add these sentences to the appropriate part of the story.

A It was pouring with rain and it was impossible to find a free taxi.

B The woman at the next table had accidentally gone off with Alice's bag.

C At the next table there was a woman, drinking a cup of tea.

D Alice at first did not notice anything but carried on reading her book.

E Just ahead of them, they could see the taxi. It had stopped at some traffic lights.

F Luckily for Alice, the woman was very friendly and offered to give her a lift in her car.

3 Write the complete story using the pictures and sentences to help you and adding any necessary details. The story must end with the sentence: *In the end, it was a very lucky day for Alice.* Write between 120 and 180 words

A

B

C

D

E

F

Photocopiable

Writing

Description (Unit 10)

1 Your suitcase was lost while you were flying back from your summer holidays. The airline has asked you to describe the suitcase and some of its contents. Look at the model description and find examples of the following language:

1 adjectives describing shape
2 adjectives describing colour
3 adjectives describing size
4 expressions describing position
5 examples of the passive voice
6 relative clauses (with which)
7 words which refer back to other parts of the text (eg it)

Description of the suitcase
The suitcase is a medium-sized brown suitcase made of leather. It is rectangular in shape and has two thick green stripes over the top and bottom. It has a zip going all the way round from the back of the suitcase to the front. The zip is fastened by a small metal lock.

The suitcase has two handles—one at the top, in the middle and a smaller one at the side, which is used for pulling the suitcase along. The case has two small wheels at one end for this purpose. On the bottom of the suitcase there is a compartment or pouch which is used for keeping documents; this also has a zip.

Description of the contents
The suitcase contains clothes, a few books and other items. The most important items of clothing are the following: two pairs of light cotton trousers, one white and the other black; one pair of blue denim shorts and one dark blue short-sleeved shirt, also made of denim. Lastly, there is a new pair of binoculars which I had bought especially for the trip.

2 Write a description of the suitcase you have lost and describe some of its contents. Read the model carefully and use the language from exercise 1 and the plan below to help you. Write between 120 and 180 words.

Paragraph 1: Appearance of the case (shape, colour, what it is made of)
Paragraph 2: Zips and handles – any other special markings
Paragraph 3: Contents (clothes)
Paragraph 4: Contents (other objects)

Writing

Article (Units 8, 11, 14)

1 Your teacher has asked your class to write an article giving an opinion on the following topic: *Is it good to be an only child?* Here are some of the things only children have said. Tick (✔) the advantages and cross (✗) the disadvantages.

> There was nobody for me to play with.

> My parents bought me a lot of presents.

> My parents never told me off.

> My parents expected me to be very special.

> My parents spent a lot of time with me.

> I always had my own bedroom.

> My parents will have only me to look after them when they are old.

> I had nobody to discuss my problems with.

> Parents spoil you.

> I learnt to be independent.

The lucky ones

Being an only child – I dream about it! I can think of so many advantages and hardly any disadvantages. The most important advantage is that you get really spoilt by everybody.

First of all, an only child has more toys than one who comes from a larger family. Parents give you whatever you ask for and you get really good presents at Christmas and for your birthday.

Secondly, an only child has his or her own bedroom and never has to share with anyone. It must be great having all that space to yourself. In addition, your parents buy you the best things for your bedroom because they want to keep you happy.

Moreover, an only child has more time with their parents. This means the child gets lots of support and help. Parents also tend to help an only child with homework more than parents with a lot of children.

Finally, an only child rarely gets told off by his or her parents. In short, an only child grows up with more love and in, in my opinion, becomes more independent.

3 Write your own answer to the question *Is it good to be an only child?* giving both advantages and disadvantages. Use the points you identified in exercise 1, the model article and the plan below to help you. Write between 120 and 180 words.

2 Read this article which explores the positive side of being an only child and answer these questions.

1 Which of the points in exercise 1 does the writer mention?
2 Tick all the points you agree with in the article.
3 Put a cross next to the points you disagree with.
4 Which connectors does the writer use?
5 Find examples of: 1) the simple present 2) modal verbs 3) phrasal verbs

Paragraph 1: Introduction
Paragraph 2: Advantages
Paragraph 3: Disadvantages
Paragraph 4: Conclusion

Remember
- use a catchy title
- begin in an interesting way
- give strong, clear arguments for or against or both
- come to a clear conclusion.

Photocopiable

Writing

Opinion/argumentative composition
(Unit 5)

1 Your teacher has asked you to write a composition on the following topic: *Mobile phones do more harm than good.* Read these statements. Tick (✔) those that are for mobile phones and cross (✗) those that are against them.

1 Doctors use them.
2 Parents can contact their children at any time.
3 They may be harmful to health.
4 You can use them while driving your car.
5 Sometimes there are no other phones available.
6 You can use them when you're away on long journeys.
7 They are expensive.
8 You can take them with you to the cinema and concerts.
9 You can talk more often to your friends.
10 You can keep in touch with important business.

2 It is important to list points using connectors. Put these connectors into a logical order by numbering them 1–13.

... because as a result	_____
Finally	_____
First of all,	_____
Of course,	_____
In my opinion / As far as I'm concerned	_____
Secondly,	_____
On the other hand,	_____
In addition,	_____
Furthermore / What's more	_____
Another point in favour/against	_____
In conclusion,	_____
On the one hand,	_____
However,	

3 Write your own composition on the subject: *Mobile phones do more harm than good.* Use the points in exercise 1, the connectors in exercise 2 and the plan below to help you. Write between 120 and 180 words.

Introduction: Your basic point of view, for or against mobile phones?
Paragraph 1: The good things about mobile phones
Paragraph 2: The problems caused by mobile phones
Conclusion: Sum up the main reason(s) why you are for or against mobile phones.

Writing

Advice/report (Unit 7)

1 A group of British students would like to go camping in your area. The group leader has asked you to write a report, answering these questions:
• where is the best place to camp in your area and why?
• what is the best time of year for camping there?
• what clothes should group members bring?
Read this model report and add the following headings to the paragraphs.

Clothing   The best time to go
Introduction   The best place to camp

A _____
The aim of this report is to describe the best place to camp in my area. It will also give visitors other useful information.
B _____
The best place is Ouzouni, which is in northern Greece. It is in a beautiful spot near the sea and it has all the essential facilities. Ouzouni is a large public campsite and it is not expensive. It has water and there are showers. There is also a restaurant and a supermarket.
C _____
The best time of year to camp at Ouzouni is in the summer months of July and August. It is an ideal time for swimming and sunbathing. Campers will also meet lots of other visitors to the area. The atmosphere is very lively.
D _____
As it is very hot at that time of year, visitors need to bring shorts, a few T-shirts and, of course, a swimming costume. In the evening it can be quite cool, so it is a good idea to bring a sweater and a pair of long trousers, for example, jeans.

2 Read the model report again and find examples of the following features of a good report:

1   saying what the aim of the report is
2   clear paragraphs

3   do not include information which is not necessary
4   give all the essential information
5   a formal or neutral style

3 Write your own report now on the best place to go for a holiday in your country. Use the model, the plan below and the useful expressions to help you. Write between 120 and 180 words.

Introduction: What is your aim?
Paragraph 1: The best place – why ?
Paragraph 2: The best time of year to go
Paragraph 3: What clothes to bring

Useful expressions

seaside	beach	coast	resort
mountain	countryside	landscape	
hotel	accommodation	cheap	
expensive	friendly	good food	
lively night-life	museums		
archeological sites	shopping		

Writing activity correction code table

Symbol	Meaning	Example
/	word missing	He went / school
?	I don't understand	We went home school ?
{	link these sentences	He didn't want to go. They made him follow them.
+	sentence/idea missing	I look forward to hearing from you. John Smith ← +
§	new paragraph needed	Dear John, Sorry I haven't written for so long. §
gr	grammar	They didn't went. **gr**
pc	punctuation	Does he play the piano, I don't know. **pc**
pr	preposition	They went in school. **pr**
R	repetition	She is very nice. She has a nice face and she is a nice girl too. **R**
S	style	Dear Sir or Madam, I read the bit about you in the newspaper. **S**
sp	spelling	He went to scool. **sp**
t	tense	I live here since 1995. **t**
wf	wrong form	We had an interest conversation. **wf**
wl	wrong linking word	Despite it was raining, they went out. **wl**
wo	word order	I like very much pop music. **wo**
ww	wrong word	My sister is a typewriter. **ww**
x	unnecesary	I must to go **x**

Practice Book answer key

1 Success!

Grammar 1

Present simple and present continuous

1 1 appears 2 is getting 3 is having
   4 do not earn 5 boils

2 1 Betty is staying with (her) friends for a few days.
   2 I spend an hour playing computer games in the evenings.
   3 Basketball is becoming more popular all the time.
   4 Debbie does not talk about her achievements much.
   5 He is preparing for the Olympics.

3 1 don't know 2 comes 3 drives
   4 is borrowing 5 spends 6 is thinking
   7 is travelling 8 own 9 believes
   10 shocks

Vocabulary 1

Personality, negative adjective prefixes

1 1 gossip 2 nervous 3 practical
   4 ambitious 5 successful 6 interesting
   7 experienced

2 1 uninteresting 2 inexpensive 3 unprofessional
   4 impolite 5 unbelievable 6 impatient
   7 independent 8 unfriendly

3 1 unbelievable 2 unfriendly 3 independent
   4 impatient 5 unsuccessful 6 impolite
   7 unprofessional 8 uninteresting 9 inexpensive

Grammar 2

Stative verbs

1 1 hate 2 believe 3 smell
   4 hear 5 forget 6 know
   7 understand 8 taste

2 1 remembers seems 2 ✓ 3 belongs to has
   4 prefer think 5 ✓ 6 knows prefers
   7 enjoys likes 8 ✓ 9 want dislike
   10 ✓

Vocabulary 2

Noun suffixes

1 1 pessimism 2 confidence 3 shyness
   4 generosity 5 curiosity 6 intelligence
   7 charm

2 1 sensitivity 2 popularity 3 confidence
   4 charm 5 politeness 6 shyness
   7 selfishness

Develop your English

1 1 B 2 C 3 D 4 A 5 D 6 B 7 A 8 D 9 C

2 1 exciting 2 unusual 3 famous
   4 interesting 5 musical 6 wealthy
   7 boring 8 expensive 9 invited
   10 boastful

2 Talking about my generation

Grammar 1

Past simple

1 1 met 2 got/switched/went
   3 saw/ran 4 loved/broke
   5 opened/came 6 started/drove
   7 arrived/remembered

2 1 B 2 A 3 C 4 D 5 C 6 D 7 A 8 D 9 C 10 B

Vocabulary 1

Clothes

1 1 hat 2 uniform 3 dressing gown
   4 overalls 5 tie 6 jumper
   7 jacket 8 trainers

2 1 skirt 2 jeans 3 shirt
   4 T-shirt 5 trousers 6 dress
   7 suit 8 jumper

Grammar 2

Past continuous

1 1 When they were growing up, they lived in the country.
   2 They fired him because of his long hair.
   3 Where was she working at the time?
   4 He did not want to have his hair cut.
   5 What was Julie wearing at the wedding?
   6 When they got to the station, the train was already leaving.
   7 People were going home when the police arrived.

2 1 it 2 ✓ 3 they
   4 been 5 ✓ 6 be
   7 as 8 did 9 ✓
   10 had 11 who 12 ✓

3 1 were trying 2 lived 3 was growing up
   4 were spending 5 were writing 6 began
   7 was wearing 8 listened 9 was doing
   10 looked

Vocabulary 2

Adjective opposites

1 1 formal 2 amusing 3 small
   4 cheap 5 expensive 6 serious
   7 noisy 8 neat 9 boring
   10 large 11 clever

2 1 fair   unfair
   2 noisy   quiet
   3 impatient patient
   4 cheap   expensive
   5 large   small
   6 interesting boring
   7 ambitious unambitious

3 1 boring 2 ambitous 3 small
   4 clever 5 interesting 6 expensive
   7 noisy 8 impatient 9 unfair
   10 cheap

Develop your English

1
1 trendy 2 miserable 3 cheerful
4 colourful 5 different 6 traditional
7 violent 8 comfortable 9 dangerous
10 expensive

2
1 dangerous 2 violent 3 cheerful
4 miserable 5 trendy 6 colourful
7 traditional 8 expensive

3
1 attractive 2 personality 3 appearance
4 useful 5 cheerful 6 colourful
7 teenagers 8 frequently 9 miserable
10 fashionable

3 Around the world

Grammar 1

Present perfect simple

1
1 She has only just come 2 I have known
3 He has never been 4 I have lived
5 I have already done

2
1 She <u>has just gone</u> to bed.
2 I <u>have had this car</u> since 1999.
3 I <u>have never been to</u> Venice before.
4 They <u>have lived in Manchester</u> for ten years.
5 She <u>still has not finished</u> her homework.

3
1 it 2 ✓ 3 been
4 ✓ 5 up 6 be
7 been 8 ✓ 9 of
10 do 11 it 12 ✓

Vocabulary 1

Compound nouns

1
1 room service 2 concert hall 3 life-style
4 news report 5 night-time 6 pencil case
7 rock star

2
1 newspaper 2 package holiday 3 night-life
4 pen friend 5 skyscrapers

Grammar 2

Present perfect continuous

1
1 has been raining 2 have eaten 3 have been running
4 have been watching 5 has fixed 6 have been cooking
7 haven't tried 8 has been learning

2
1 have been 2 have been having 3 have spent
4 have never visited 5 have been 6 haven't seen
7 have walked 8 has been raining 9 have been writing
10 has been going

3 1 A 2 C 3 D 4 C 5 B 6 A 7 A

Vocabulary 2

Travel

1 1 h 2 c 3 g 4 e 5 a 6 b 7 d 8 i

2
1 campsite 2 luggage 3 packed our cases
4 return ticket 5 timetable 6 queue
7 platform 8 motorway 9 miss a bus

3
1 port 2 cabin 3 reserve
4 miss 5 turbulence 6 aeroplane
7 underground 8 deck 9 guard
10 tourist

Develop your English

1
1 success 2 tourist 3 employment
4 allowance 5 population 6 explanation
7 inspiration 8 performance 9 celebration
10 inhabitant

2
1 traditional 2 musical 3 theatrical
4 beautiful 5 charming 6 fashionable
7 different 8 famous 9 mysterious
10 romantic

3
1 inspiration 2 performance 3 allowance
4 different 5 musical 6 traditional
7 famous 8 population

4
1 arrival 2 beautiful 3 population
4 inhabitants 5 nationalities 6 tourists
7 especially 8 visitors 9 wonderful
10 enthusiastic 11 charming

4 A touch of magic

Grammar 1

Past perfect simple

1
1 had forgotten 2 had caught 3 had left
4 had started 5 had seen

2
1 She <u>had been to</u> Prague before.
2 They <u>had studied very hard</u> before taking the test.
3 The film <u>had started</u> by the time they got there.
4 She had to borrow some money because <u>she had lost</u> her purse.
5 She <u>had been asleep</u> for an hour when the noise woke her up.

Vocabulary 1

Noun suffixes

1
1 art 2 journalist 3 sailor
4 magic 5 performer 6 producing
7 reporter 8 pianist

2
1 magician 2 sailor 3 performer
4 artist 5 politician

Grammar 2

Past perfect continuous, *used to* and *would*

1
1 been 2 had 3 was
4 went 5 been 6 spoken
7 leave 8 had 9 had
10 told 11 wait 12 had
13 searched 14 find

2
1 had been taking 2 had stolen 3 used to speak
4 used to eat 5 had been snowing 6 had grown
7 would tell

3 1 ✓ 2 been 3 being
4 ✓ 5 will 6 have
7 have 8 being 9 never
10 ✓

Vocabulary 2

Adjective suffixes

1 1 boring 2 depressed 3 interested
4 surprising 5 disappointing 6 exciting
7 excited

2 1 dangerous 2 idiotic 3 marvellous
4 shiny 5 selective

Develop your English

1 1 believed 2 unforgettable 3 foolish
4 scientific 5 mysterious 6 interesting
7 reporter 8 amazing 9 astonishing

2 1 D 2 D 3 B 4 C 5 B 6 B 7 A 8 A 9 C

3 1 show 2 natural 3 reporter
4 excitement 5 understand 6 performance
7 astonished 8 actor 9 laugh
10 recognize 11 take in 12 unbelievable

5 Them and us

Grammar 1

Comparatives and superlatives: adjectives

1 1 The most difficult subject at school is …
2 The best swimmer in my family is …
3 The worst test result I have ever had is …
4 The highest building in my town is …
5 The happiest moment in my life was …
6 The oldest thing I own is ..
7 The most valuable thing I own is …
8 The smallest thing I have in my pocket is …

2 1 May is our busiest time of year.
2 Nobody in the class is more intelligent than Debbie.
3 She is the best actress in Hollywood.
4 This is the worst composition I have ever seen.
5 Frankfurt is bigger than Munich.
6 Jenny is a more careful driver than John.
7 My Italian is better than my Greek.
8 He is the fastest runner in the world.

3 1 Jill is more mature than Sue.
2 John is more competitive than Bob.
3 Jim's jokes are funnier than Fred's.
4 Albert is more intelligent than Charles.
5 Yesterday's test was more difficult than today's.
6 Sheila ran faster than Peter.
7 Rome is more beautiful than Coketown.

4 1 in 2 of 3 than
4 most 5 on 6 much
7 than 8 best 9 fastest

Vocabulary 1

Feelings

1 1 proud 2 jealous 3 upset
4 pleased 5 embarrassed 6 afraid
7 ashamed

2 1 afraid 2 proud 3 jealous
4 ashamed 5 upset

Grammar 2

Comparatives and superlatives: adverbs

1 1 Please drive more carefully.
2 Your sister keeps her room tidier than you do.
3 The boys who worked the hardest won prizes.
4 Try to come sooner than two o'clock.
5 Answer the easiest question first.

2 1 ✓ 2 more 3 ✓
4 much 5 a 6 ✓
7 more 8 more 9 that
10 ✓

Vocabulary 2

Relationships

1 1 get on (with) 2 go off 3 break up (with)
4 be crazy about 5 be close to 6 fall out (with)

2 1 broke up 2 fancied 3 have a date
4 going out 5 was crazy about 6 were close to
7 got on 8 had a row 9 separate
10 had fallen in love

Develop your English

1 1 D 2 B 3 C 4 A 5 C 6 D 7 B 8 C

2 1 competitive 2 intelligent 3 annoying
4 irritating 5 friendly 6 noisy
7 proud 8 surprising

3 1 intelligent 2 best 3 unusual
4 talented 5 proud 6 competition
7 well 8 noisy 9 irritating

4 1 friendly 2 row 3 noisy
4 separate 5 depend 6 embarrassed
7 upset 8 happy 9 intelligent
10 personality

6 Starstruck

Grammar 1

Future simple and *going to*

1
1. I will lend you my bicycle, but please ride it carefully.
2. The new manager is going to make a lot of changes to the company.
3. When I finish university I am going to travel round the world.
4. I will do the washing up while you go and lie down.
5. I think it is going to rain.

2
1 will	2 are going to	3 will
4 will	5 will	6 will
7 are going to	8 are going to	9 won't

Vocabulary 1

Noun suffixes

1
1 prediction	2 explosion	3 decision
4 revolution	5 qualification	6 destruction
7 explanation	8 communication	

2
1 prediction	2 qualification	3 explanation
4 decision	5 communication	

Grammar 2

Present continuous and present simple (for future)

1
1 am flying	2 leaves	3 am not going
4 are	5 will you finish	6 are you doing

2
1. Jenny is visiting/is going to visit her grandmother on Saturday.
2. I am working/am going to work at home tomorrow.
3. Tomorrow is Friday 7 April.
4. We are getting married/are going to get married on Saturday.

3
1 been	2 ✓	3 it
4 ✓	5 much	6 have
7 for	8 and	9 will
10 to		

Vocabulary 2

Collocations and phrasal verbs with *set*

1
1 up	2 on	3 out
4 the table	5 the clock	6 fire
7 a good example	8 foot	9 free

2
1 trap	2 sail	3 heart
4 record	5 foot	6 dinner
7 off	8 example	9 fire
10 free		

Develop your English

1 1 A 2 C 3 D 4 B 5 C 6 D 7 D 8 A 9 B

2
1 recently	2 invention	3 interesting
4 transformed	5 disagree	6 disadvantages
7 noisy	8 pollution	9 entertainment
10 relaxing	11 educational	

7 Terrors of the earth and sky

Grammar 1

Modal verbs

1 1 g 2 h 3 b 4 c 5 e 6 d 7 a

2
1. That volcano will erupt: I am sure of it.
2. She must be hungry if she had no breakfast.
3. You mustn't eat or drink in class.
4. A parrot can only copy sounds, which is not the same as talking.
5. The tickets may be more than £10 each, so take some extra money.
6. They should get here at about nine o'clock.
7. She can't be ill.

Vocabulary 1

Homonyms

1
1 rock	2 branch	3 bark
4 leaves	5 force	6 rock
7 leaves	8 branch	9 force
10 bark		

2 1 h, m   2 e, n   3 g, o   4 c, i   5 k, p   6 d, j   7 a, l

3
1 coach	2 bank	3 rock
4 hand	5 head	6 branch
7 trunk	8 land	

Grammar 2

Modal verbs and modal perfect

1
1 need	2 should/ought to
3 can't	4 should/ought to
5 don't have to/needn't	6 should/ought to
7 can/may	8 have to/must

2
1 must have rained	2 can't have stolen
3 may/might have been	4 may have arrived
5 can't have broken	6 must have worked

3
1 the	2 ✓	3 to
4 to	5 ✓	6 they
7 ✓	8 to	9 and
10 to	11 of	

Vocabulary 2

Environment

1 1 C 2 B 3 A 4 B 5 A 6 D 7 D 8 C

2
1 recycle	2 newspapers	3 vibration
4 international	5 erupt	6 ozone layer
7 genetic	8 measures	9 endangered
10 nuclear energy	11 tap	

Develop your English

1
1 can	2 should	3 can
4 should	5 can	6 ought
7 should	8 have	9 should
10 need		

2
1	information	2	eruption	3	destruction

2
1 information 2 eruption 3 destruction
4 protection 5 instruction 6 prevention
7 organization 8 container 9 suggestion
10 production.
The different noun is <u>container</u>.

3
1 organization 2 suggestions 3 destruction
4 information 5 container 6 instructions
7 eruption 8 prevention

4
1 global 2 information 3 situation
4 pollution 5 dangerous 6 international
7 possibility 8 recycle 9 natural
10 obligation 11 protection

8 The happiest days?

Grammar 1

First and second conditionals

1
1 d 2 b 3 h 4 g 5 c 6 e 7 j 8 i

2
1 If I have time this weekend, I will …
2 If I lived in Argentina, I would speak Spanish.
3 If my friend asks me to go to the cinema this evening, I will say …
4 If I found a wallet full of money, I would …
5 If I had the chance, I would like to visit…
6 If I pass all my exams this year, I will …

3
1 would 2 had 3 spend
4 get 5 do 6 will
7 carry 8 have 9 were
10 will 11 relax 12 would

Vocabulary 1

Common verbs

1
1 get 2 say 3 have
4 want 5 think 6 go
7 Take

2
1 Take 2 get 3 want
4 Think 5 have 6 Say
7 Go

Grammar 2

Zero conditional

1
1 will get 2 melts 3 would go
4 switch off 5 will buy 6 would buy
7 hurts 8 feel

2
1 These trousers <u>would fit me</u> if I were slimmer.
2 She <u>will be surprised</u> if she passes her exams.
3 If <u>you boil</u> vegetables for too long, they will lose their flavour.
4 If you go shopping, I <u>will do</u> the cooking.
5 If I wanted you to come with me, I <u>would tell you</u>.
6 If <u>you listen to music</u> while you work, you will feel relaxed.
7 If I were you, I <u>would see</u> a doctor about your backache.

Vocabulary 2

Collocations with common verbs

1
1 do 2 make 3 do
4 making 5 made 6 do
7 do 8 make

2
1 go ahead 2 go off 3 go back
4 go away 5 get by 6 get over

3
1 got over 2 went back 3 got away
4 get by 5 gone off 6 go ahead

Develop your English

1
1 had 2 it 3 ✔
4 did 5 of 6 ✔
7 of 8 ✔ 9 much
10 will

2
1 B 2 A 3 C 4 D 5 B 6 D 7 A 8 A 9 C 10 D
11 A 12 C

3
1 comparisons 2 children 3 generation
4 education 5 harder 6 disagree
7 revising 8 examinations 9 exaggeration
10 forgotten 11 misbehave

4
1 popular 2 learn 3 mathematics
4 university 5 geography 6 breaks
7 joke 8 plumber 9 nurse
10 holidays

9 What a laugh!

Grammar 1

1
1 h 2 d 3 g 4 a 5 f 6 c 7 b 8 e

2
1 If her vocabulary <u>had been better</u>, she wouldn't have made the mistake.
2 If she <u>had stopped at</u> the red light, she would have passed her driving test.
3 If we <u>had arrived on/in time</u>, we wouldn't have missed the start of the film.
4 We <u>would have gone to</u> Paris if we had had enough money.
5 If I had known Spanish, I <u>would have enjoyed my holiday</u> more.
6 She <u>would not have married</u> Peter if she hadn't felt lonely.

Vocabulary 1

Word formation

1
1 laughing 2 happiest 3 laughable
4 laugh 5 unhappy 6 laughter
7 happiness

2
1 success successful successfully unsuccessful unsuccessfully succeeding succeeded
2 failure failing unfailing unfailingly failed

Grammar 2

Wish and *if only*

1
1 had eaten 2 would have asked
3 hadn't been sent off 4 would have got
5 knew 6 had worked
7 wouldn't chew 8 could dance

2
1 I wish/If only I hadn't driven so fast.
2 I wish/If only I knew how to swim.
3 I wish/If only I hadn't stayed late at the party.
4 I wish/If only I played a musical instrument.
5 I wish/If only you would stop annoying your sister.

3 1 they   2 ✔   3 have
4 the   5 ✔   6 he
7 ✔   8 too   9 ✔
10 had   11 got

Vocabulary 2

Colours

1 1 green with envy   2 blue with cold
3 white as a sheet   4 red as a beetroot

2 1 f   2 a   3 d   4 e   5 c   6 b

Develop your English

1 1 had   2 came   3 been
4 when   5 used   6 was
7 the   8 told   9 for
10 later   11 of   12 when

2 1 funny   2 amusement amusing
3 laugh laughter   4 joke
5 smile smiling   6 humour

3 1 funny/amusing/humorous   2 joke
3 Smile   4 humour
5 laughter   6 fun

4 1 laughter   2 healthy   3 pleasant
4 knowledge   5 variety   6 amusing
7 funny   8 gardening   9 activities

5 1 B   2 A   3 B   4 C   5 B   6 C   7 D   8 A   9 D

10 A question of difference

Grammar 1

The passive

2 1 The bank has been robbed.
2 All the money was taken from the cashier.
3 A man is being questioned by the police.
4 Robberies are reported in the newspapers every day.
5 The police are blamed for the increase in crime.
6 Measures will be taken by the police to reduce crime.
7 Anyone who looks suspicious will be stopped by the police.

3 1 English <u>is spoken in</u> most of the hotels.
2 My pocket calculator <u>was broken by</u> my sister.
3 The money <u>has been taken</u> from the box.
4 The bridge <u>will be repaired</u> as soon as possible.
5 It <u>is believed</u> that the thief was a local man.
6 Her <u>portrait was painted by</u> Picasso.
7 The flat <u>has not been decorated</u> for ten years.

Vocabulary 1

Collective nouns

1 1 a flock of sheep   2 a herd of elephants
3 a team of athletes   4 a pile of rubbish
5 a crowd of people   6 a bunch of flowers

2 1 pile   2 herd   3 pack
4 gang   5 bunch   6 set

Grammar 2

The causative

1 1 I've never had my eyesight checked.
2 I'm having my shoes mended on Monday.
3 I had a cake made for my sister's birthday.
4 I've just had the car repaired.
5 I'm going to have the outside of the house painted yellow.

2 1 I'm going to have my hair cut.
2 I've just had a tooth taken out.
3 I've just had my car washed.
4 She had breakfast cooked for her.

3 1 ✔   2 be   3 been
4 the   5 been   6 ✔
7 the   8 they   9 been
10 to   11 up   12 ✔

Vocabulary 2

Arts and sciences

1 1 writing   2 pen   3 manuscripts
4 science   5 architecture   6 building
7 paintbrush

2 1 ruins   2 manuscripts   3 telescope
4 sculpture   5 writer   6 formulae
7 mathematics   8 pen   9 science
10 astronomer

Develop your English

1 1 ago   2 been   3 is
4 his   5 were   6 not
7 by   8 had   9 was
10 been   11 where   12 by
13 will   14 were

2 1 twentieth   2 important   3 readers
4 majority   5 explorer   6 discovery
7 artist   8 certainly   9 paintings
10 inventions

3 1 D   2 A   3 D   4 B   5 D   6 C   7 B   8 D

11 The fight for freedom

Grammar 1

Relative clauses: *who, whose, which*

1 1 who   2 who   3 which
4 whose   5 whose   6 who
7 which   8 which

2 1 Children <u>who eat too many chocolates</u> can get bad teeth.
2 Pizza, <u>which is my favourite food</u>, comes from Italy.
3 The people <u>who saw the film</u> liked it a lot.
4 Mercouri, <u>who fought for democracy</u>, was not only an actress but a politician too.
5 The First World War, <u>which broke out in 1914</u>, ended in 1918.
6 That woman, <u>whose name I have forgotten</u>, lives near here.

3 1 That's the athlete who won a gold medal.
   2 That's the bus which we have to catch.
   3 That's the girl whose book you borrowed.
   4 That's the politician who spoke at the meeting..
   5 That's the road which leads to Rome.

Vocabulary 1

Nouns with and without the definite article

1 1 ✗   2 a   3 ✗
   4 ✗   5 a   6 ✗
   7 ✗   8 a   9 a
   10 ✗   11 an   12 the

2 1 to Seward Road   2 to work   3 in England

Grammar 2

Relative clauses: *when* and *where*

1 1 when   2 where   3 when
   4 where   5 where   6 when
   7 when   8 where

2 1 it   2 ✓   3 do
   4 ✓   5 does   6 who
   7 who   8 ✓   9 whose
   10 ✓   11 the   12 ✓
   13 where   14 ✓

Vocabulary 2

Noun suffixes

1 1 gangster   2 leader   3 celebrity
   4 murderer   5 millionaire   6 musician
   7 blackmailer   8 politician   9 terrorist
   10 dictator

2 1 celebrities   2 millionaire   3 musicians
   4 gangsters   5 terrorists   6 dictators
   7 murderer   8 Leaders

Develop your English

1 1 A 2 C 3 B 4 C 5 B 6 D 7 A 8 D 9 C 10 B
   11 A 12 C 13 D

2 1 of/from   2 was   3 which
   4 to   5 in   6 which
   7 about   8 over   9 for
   10 who   11 of   12 to
   13 to

3 1 organizations   2 attention   3 prisoners
   4 beliefs   5 publicity   6 unknown
   7 children   8 terrible   9 freedom
   10 democratic

4 1 heroes   2 outstanding   3 member
   4 democracy   5 conscience   6 religion
   7 prison   8 fight   9 hungry
   10 charity   11 protest

12 Life in the 21st century

Grammar 1

Future perfect simple

1 1 In ten years' time, everyone <u>will have learnt to use</u> the internet.
   2 We <u>will have lived here</u> for three years by next month.
   3 They <u>will not have finished</u> the new robot until 2020.
   4 By the end of this term, we <u>will have taken</u> five tests.
   5 By ten o'clock, I <u>will have done</u> all my homework.
   6 The temperature <u>will have reached</u> 40°C by the end of July.

2 1 will have disappeared   2 will have created
   3 will have been   4 will have appeared
   5 will have developed   6 will have become
   7 will have replaced   8 will have become

Vocabulary 1

Phrasal verbs with *up*

1 1 made up g   2 get up c   3 look up a
   4 bring up f   5 turned up e   6 gave up b

2 1 turn up   2 brought up   3 looked up
   4 made up   5 give up   6 gets up
   7 came up

Grammar 2

Future continuous

1 1 We <u>will be going</u> on a one-day excursion on Friday.
   2 I <u>will be taking</u> a test at that time, so I can't come.
   3 This time tomorrow, I <u>will be sailing</u> in the Aegean.
   4 Next year, I <u>will be learning to drive</u>.

2 1 will be swimming   2 will be going
   3 will have spent   4 will have lost

3 1 to   2 yet   3 ✓
   4 ✓   5 to   6 a
   7 will   8 to   9 ✓
   10 ✓   11 the   12 gone
   13 the   14 ✓

Vocabulary 2

Phrasal verbs

1 1 carry on   2 carry out   3 get back
   4 get away   5 get on   6 turn into
   7 find out

2 1 turns into   2 found out   3 carrying out
   4 carry on   5 set off   6 get away
   7 get back   8 get on

3 1 get back   2 set off   3 get on
   4 turn into   5 find out   6 carry on
   7 get out   8 get away

Develop your English

1 1 B 2 C 3 A 4 B 5 D 6 A 7 C 8 D 9 B 10 C
   11 A 12 D 13 A 14 C 15 B

2
1	behaviour	2	information	3	speech
4	appearance	5	entertainment	6	belief
7	embarrassment	8	feeling	9	reaction
10	life	11	generation	12	prediction
13	solution				

3
1	entertainment	2	appearance	3	information
4	lives	5	feelings	6	generation
7	speech	8	behaviour	9	solution
10	belief	11	reactions		

13 I spy ...

Grammar 1

Reported speech: tense changes

1
1 He told them he <u>earned money</u> by writing.
2 She said she <u>was going back</u> to Paris on Monday.
3 She told me she <u>had done</u> her homework.
4 She said <u>(that) she preferred</u> Sean Connery to Roger Moore.
5 He told us <u>(that) he had read every</u> one of the James Bond books.
6 Moore told the reporter he <u>had played/taken the part</u> of Hamlet when he was at school.
7 The scientist <u>told us he was working</u> on a new drug.
8 She said she thought <u>there was too much violence</u> on television.

2
1	had been	2	had been	3	had had
4	had been	5	felt	6	had never forgotten
7	had visited	8	had met	9	was planning
10	was going				

Vocabulary 1

Phrasal verbs with *take*

1
1	takes after	2	couldn't take in	3	took down
4	took to	5	has taken on	6	is taking up

2
1	down	2	in	3	up
4	after	5	on	6	to

Grammar 2

Reported speech: other changes

1
1 You told me you <u>would do it the next</u> day.
2 She <u>told us to take those</u> with us.
3 They warned <u>that they might leave</u> early.
4 My dad said <u>he could do it then</u>.
5 He said he <u>had to go to</u> the dentist the next day.
6 The reporter said he <u>could not tell that</u> to anyone.
7 They said they <u>did not want to go</u> up in the lift.
8 The police officer said he <u>would not tell me/us another</u> time.

2
1 'Make me some tea, please,' Pond said to Honeybunch.
2 'This is exactly what we will need,' he agreed.
3 'I must meet him tomorrow,' she said.
4 'You can't put your bag here,' he said to me.
5 'Don't leave your watches in the classroom,' the teacher said to us.
6 'I might see a ballet at the Bolshoi,' Pond said to me.

Vocabulary 2

Narrative styles

1
1	make an arrest	2	commit murder		
3	set off early	4	violent criminal		
5	check-in desk	6	creaky door		
7	spooky atmosphere	8	late arrival		
9	heavy suitcase	10	haunted house		

2
1	violent criminal	2	haunted house		
3	late arrival	4	spooky atmosphere		
5	check-in desk	6	heavy suitcase		
7	make an arrest	8	creaky door		
9	set off early	10	commit murder		

Develop your English

1
1	by	2	of	3	up
4	old	5	when	6	over
7	of	8	had	9	on
10	not	11	made	12	took/made
13	back	14	although		

2 1 B 2 B 3 C 4 D 5 A 6 B 7 C 8 D 9 A 10 A
11 B 12 A 13 C 14 D 15 B

3
1	it	2	✓	3	for
4	she	5	✓	6	to
7	to	8	from	9	✓
10	he	11	✓	12	have
13	was	14	✓		

4
1	dangerous	2	founder	3	wealthy
4	variety	5	producer	6	powerful
7	friendly/friends	8	threatened	9	influential
10	instructions	11	activities		

14 Art and artists

Grammar 1

Reported questions

1 1 g 2 d 3 e 4 b 5 f 6 a 7 c

2
1	if/whether	2	had been	3	made
4	was	5	when	6	would
7	what	8	began	9	had
10	was	11	had	12	asked

3
1 She asked me if/whether I knew where the post office was.
2 The policeman enquired where I/we got the money.
3 He asked me why I was late.
4 My brother wondered if/whether it was raining again.
5 He wanted to know if/whether I/we had ever met anyone famous.

4
1 He asked me whether I had ever been to London.
2 They wanted to know who it was.
3 I asked her to tell me her phone number.
4 She wanted to know why I wanted it.
5 The doctor asked me if I was feeling tired.
6 I asked the doctor what was wrong with me.

Vocabulary 1

Verb + preposition

1 1 listen to   2 worry about   3 succeed in
   4 take part in   5 think about   6 believe in
   7 arrive in   8 go to

2 1 think about   2 talk to   3 arrived in
   4 go to   5 succeed in   6 worry about
   7 take part in   8 listen to

Grammar 2

Indirect questions

1 1 Do you mind telling me where you come from?
   2 Have you any idea how he does that?
   3 Could I ask if/whether you have got a ticket?
   4 Do you know if we can do it again?
   5 Could you tell me where you learnt to speak English?

2 1 Can I ask you how far it is to Athens?
   2 Could you tell me why you are here at this time of night?
   3 Can you tell me where you are going?
   4 Have you any idea how busy I am now?

Vocabulary 2

Adjective + preposition

1 1 keen on   2 interested in   3 good at
   4 famous for   5 sorry for   6 angry about
   7 excited about   8 happy about   9 proud of
   10 tired of   11 fond of

2 1 proud of   2 interested in   3 good at
   4 angry about   5 happy about   6 keen on
   7 excited about   8 famous for

Develop your English

1 1 A   2 C   3 D   4 A   5 B   6 C   7 A   8 B   9 D   10 C

2 1 ✓   2 of   3 ✓
   4 to   5 a   6 had
   7 ✓   8 been   9 more
   10 ✓   11 for   12 ✓
   13 am   14 do

3 1 exhibition   2 introduction
   3 interesting   4 paintings
   5 artists   6 explanation(s)
   7 description   8 meant
   9 pleasure   10 personally
   11 revelation

15 Our wonderful world

Grammar 1

Time clauses

1 1 comes   2 get   3 tells
   4 passes   5 leave   6 takes

2 1 I'll send you an e-mail <u>as soon as I get</u> home.
   2 We won't go sightseeing <u>before we check into</u> the hotel.

3 We can't buy a house <u>until we have</u> enough money.
   4 Why don't we have a coffee <u>while we wait/are waiting</u> for John?
   5 The film will be over <u>by the time we get</u> there.

Vocabulary 1

Noun + preposition

1 1 talk on   2 reply to   3 qualification in
   4 expert on   5 description of   6 reason for

2 1 There was a really good description of the concert in the paper yesterday.
   2 My grandmother has just got her qualifications in diving.
   3 The dog had a good reason for biting the postman.
   4 Is there any information about birds in that book?
   5 The headteacher is giving a talk on the new school building tomorrow.

Grammar 2

Infinitives and gerunds

1 1 to clean   2 walking   3 cry
   4 to be   5 posting   6 to rent
   7 having   8 have   9 to paint
   10 doing

2 1 I'd rather   2 you'd better   3 succeed in
   4 manage to   5 don't mind   6 can't stand
   7 make   8 let   9 arrive at
   10 refuse to   11 deny

3 1 to join   2 to go   3 to pay
   4 to do   5 running   6 swimming
   7 to start   8 being   9 doing

Vocabulary 2

Animals

1 1 elephant   2 dove   3 bear
   4 dolphin   5 camel   6 hawk
   7 cockroach   8 eagle   9 butterfly
   10 zebra

2 across: mosquito camel lion monkey snake
   down: seal bee hawk bear
   diagonally: eagle ant spider
   backwards: tiger zebra

Develop your English

1 1 to   2 leaves   3 looking
   4 up   5 used   6 go
   7 spend   8 soon   9 takes/gets
   10 out   11 until   12 to
   13 time   14 mind   15 up

2 1 B   2 D   3 A   4 D   5 C   6 B   7 C   8 A   9 D   10 D

3 1 ✓   2 the   3 to
   4 ✓   5 be   6 ✓
   7 to   8 at   9 to
   10 ✓   11 not   12 to

4 1 survival   2 hunters   3 illegal
   4 dumping   5 investigations   6 responsible
   7 punishment   8 behaviour   9 threatens
   10 products   11 solution

Test Booklet answer key

- Students' own answers – those given are suggestions only

Progress test 1

1 Grammar

1	is recording	2	appears	3	is having
4	lives	5	start	6	prefers
7	are getting	8	are having	9	ride
10	goes				

2 Grammar

1	do you usually start	2	do you go	3	belongs
4	understand	5	is she running	6	is not enjoying
7	tastes	8	are making	9	think
10	it's raining				

3 Grammar *

1 Do you like paintings?
2 How do you spend/What do you do in your free time?
3 What are you reading?
4 Where does she work?
5 Is he learning to play a musical instrument?
6 When's your birthday?
7 What time/When do they usually go to bed?
8 Do you have/own a car?
9 Do you know what the word means?/What does the word mean?
10 Do you like the Spice Girls?

4 Vocabulary

1	funny	2	ambitious	3	inexperienced
4	unusual	5	nervous	6	inexpensive
7	aggressive	8	impractical	9	unsuccessful
10	dull				

5 Vocabulary

1 d   2 h   3 e   4 j   5 i   6 g   7 a   8 b   9 f   10 c

Progress test 2

1 Grammar

1	wore	2	warned	3	got
4	denied	5	put	6	played
7	had	8	said	9	was
10	liked				

2 Grammar

1	was wearing	2	needed	3	was shining
4	failed	5	were watching	6	went
7	was taking	8	lived	9	arrived
10	was playing				

3 Error correction

1	did she wear	2	did it start	3	were you doing
4	Was it snowing	5	did he wear	6	Were you
7	was it	8	did you wake up	9	Was he reading
10	did you enjoy				

4 Vocabulary

1	uniform	2	suit	3	tie
4	overalls	5	jumper	6	T-shirt
7	dress	8	jeans	9	trainers
10	skirt				

5 Vocabulary

1	interesting	2	formal	3	noisy
4	cheap	5	small	6	tall
7	untidy	8	stupid	9	unfair
10	funny				

Progress test 3

1 Key word transformations

1 I have been playing the guitar since I was sixteen.
2 They have never been to the Greek islands before.
3 She has just arrived.
4 We have already been to a rock concert.
5 I have not finished tidying my room yet.
6 He has been living here for two years.
7 She still has not phoned her mother.
8 I have been writing this letter for a week.
9 It has been snowing since this morning.
10 Tourists have been coming to Ibiza since the 60s.

2 Grammar

1	just	2	since	3	already
4	still	5	never	6	ever
7	yet	8	for	9	since
10	just				

3 Error Correction

1	have you lived	2	has been raining	3	have never seen
4	hasn't heard	5	haven't finished	6	have been waiting
7	has it been snowing	8	have already seen	9	done their homework yet
10	have you been waiting				

4 Vocabulary

1	package	2	night	3	tourist
4	news	5	rock	6	pen
7	hotel	8	sky	9	back
10	fore				

5 Vocabulary

1	A	2	D	3	B
4	B	5	C	6	D
7	C	8	C	9	A
10	D				

Progress test 4

1 Grammar

1	had gone	2	had lost	3	had not finished
4	had been playing	5	had never gone	6	had been driving
7	had not eaten	8	had been practising	9	had disappeared
10	had been performing				

2 Grammar

1	had been waiting	2	had failed	3	would protest
4	played	5	had been standing	6	had been snowing
7	had you been studying			8	hadn't finished
9	was pulling	10	used to enjoy		

3 Word formation

1	politicians	2	performer	3	scientists
4	journalist	5	magician	6	driver
7	reporter	8	artists	9	competitor
10	sailor				

4 Vocabulary

1 excited	2 mysterious	3 brilliant
4 foolish	5 funny	6 disappointed
7 jealous	8 boring	9 creative
10 surprised		

5 Vocabulary

1 C	2 B	3 C
4 D	5 A	6 B
7 B	8 C	9 D
10 B		

Progress test 5

1 Grammar

1 C	2 D	3 A
4 D	5 C	6 B
7 A	8 D	9 B
10 D		

2 Key word transformations

1 Anthony <u>drives more slowly than</u> Michael.
2 Pupils take maths <u>more seriously than</u> English.
3 Maria <u>works harder in the morning</u> than in the evening.
4 Some boys <u>cook better than</u> girls.
5 Men <u>speak more loudly than</u> women.
6 Anthony finished <u>the test sooner than</u> anyone else.
7 You'll <u>get there more quickly</u> if you by air.
8 Marion Jones <u>is the fastest runner</u> in the world.
9 She <u>writes worse than anyone</u> else in the class.
10 If you write <u>more carefully,</u> you won't make so many mistakes.

3 Vocabulary

1 serious	2 afraid	3 proud
4 jealous	5 attracted	6 upset
7 ashamed	8 confident	9 embarrassed
10 friendly		

4 Vocabulary

1 b   2 d   3 h   4 a   5 i   6 e   7 f   8 j   9 g   10 c

5 Vocabulary *

1 Don't boast about how good you are at everything.
2 We're very good friends and we get on very well.
3 She was very supportive and helped me solve my problems.
4 She thinks she is always right and doesn't like criticism.
5 Tim always wants to be the best – he's very competitive.
6 I was so tired that I couldn't go on, so we stopped to have a rest.
7 Why blame the boy when he didn't do it?
8 He gets embarrassed when you tease him.
9 The car is making a very irritating noise and I must take it to a garage.
10 We had a friendly chat about the situation.

Progress test 6

1 Grammar

1 will	2 am going to	3 will
4 will	5 will	6 is going to
7 will	8 am going to	9 is going to
10 will		

2 Grammar

1 am going to	2 leaves	3 are having
4 begins	5 is going to	6 am flying
7 have	8 is going to rain	9 will give
10 takes off		

3 Error correction

1 to	2 for	3 it
4 be	5 give	6 will
7 away	8 on	9 a
10 the		

4 Word formation

1 pollution	2 education	3 predictions
4 description	5 observation	6 permission
7 revision	8 invention	9 construction
10 possession		

5 Vocabulary

1 record	2 foot	3 free
4 date	5 sail/off	6 heart
7 trap	8 example	9 fire
10 table		

Progress test 7

1 Grammar

1 B	2 C	3 D
4 C	5 A	6 B
7 D	8 D	9 A
10 B		

2 Key word transformations

1 Students at university <u>may miss some lessons.</u>
2 You <u>should write her a letter.</u>
3 I <u>must lose weight.</u>
4 You <u>have to be sixteen</u> to take part in the competition.
5 You <u>need your books to go</u> to school.
6 We <u>don't have to</u> book seats before we go.
7 We <u>couldn't stay in/inside</u> the house.
8 You <u>ought to drive more carefully.</u>
9 You <u>don't have to be</u> back by midnight.
10 She <u>can't be from Argentina.</u>

3 Error correction

1 may have started	2 must have been	3 can't have closed
4 may have been	5 don't have to	6 must try
7 may have	8 should	9 can't have lost
10 ought to take		

4 Vocabulary

1 branch	2 bark	3 ground
4 ground	5 branch	6 bark
7 roots	8 leaves	9 rock
10 leaves		

5 Vocabulary

1 warming	2 tropical	3 layer
4 cans	5 pollution	6 dumping
7 ban	8 endangered	9 close
10 save		

Progress test 8

1 Key word transformations

1 If <u>you visit Egypt,</u> you will see the pyramids.
2 If <u>I had the money,</u> I'd buy a new computer.
3 I'll have more space <u>if I buy</u> a new flat.
4 If you won first prize, <u>you would get</u> a brand new car.
5 If you go to London, <u>you will probably see</u> Trafalgar Square.
6 If I knew Chinese, <u>I would be able</u> to read this book.
7 If <u>you do a lot of</u> exercise, you lose weight.
8 If you like swimming, <u>you should spend your holidays</u> on an island.
9 If <u>you don't keep ice</u> in the fridge, it melts.
10 If <u>I had time,</u> I'd go to the concert.

2 Grammar *

1 you'll feel tired   2 it melts.   3 go to the doctor.
4 you can go home. 5 they feel good.   6 you'll eat hamburgers
7 I'd say hello   8 it rained more   9 the teacher made jokes.
10 I pass this exam.

3 Grammar

1 i   2 d   3 f   4 e   5 b   6 g   7 c   8 j   9 a   10 h

4 Vocabulary

1 do the housework   2 make/get a phone call
3 have a chat   4 have a holiday   5 do your best
6 have an idea   7 have a rest   8 have/make lunch
9 have/make friends   10 do/get a job

5 Vocabulary

1 get away   2 go ahead   3 get by
4 go off   5 go back   6 get over
7 go out   8 go off   9 get on
10 get on

Progress test 9

1 Key word transformations

1 I would have caught the train if I had gone to the right platform.
2 If the man had spoken English, someone would have understood him.
3 She wouldn't have lost a lot of weight if she hadn't stopped eating bread.
4 If he hadn't worked hard, he wouldn't have passed his exams.
5 He wouldn't have started to learn English if he hadn't wanted to travel.
6 If the croissants had been hot, we would have enjoyed them.
7 If only I could drive a car!
8 I wish I had accepted their offer of a job.
9 If you had come on holiday with us, it would have been nicer.
10 If only I didn't make so many mistakes in tests!

2 Grammar

1 had studied   2 had not forgotten   3 would have become
4 wouldn't have got 5 had worn   6 didn't tell
7 would help   8 didn't talk   9 would be
10 had not made

3 Vocabulary

1 laughing   2 laughed   3 laughter
4 unhappy   5 happiest   6 Happiness
7 happy   8 happily   9 laughable
10 laugh

4 Vocabulary

1 white   2 black   3 blue
4 red   5 blue   6 green
7 bright   8 dark   9 pale
10 Green

5 Vocabulary *

1 How often do you attend English lessons?
2 The staff at the school include ten teachers and the director.
3 My colleague, John, is the person I get on with best at work.
4 I am determined to get my certificate – nothing will stop me!
5 I asked if she wanted to come with me and she gave a nod.
6 He wanted to take care of sick animals.
7 She was a graduate from the university.
8 The canoe had two paddles.
9 They went up the river in a canoe.
10 The lion tamer used a whip to control the lion.

Progress test 10

1 Grammar

1 He was accused of the murder by the police.
2 Two other murders are being investigated.
3 The water is put into the saucepan and boiled.
4 Helen's bag has been stolen.
5 He was given a new computer for his birthday by his parents.
6 The pizza had been made that morning.
7 *Great Expectations* and *A Tale of Two Cities* were written by Dickens.
8 The new bridge will be finished by next month.
9 The novels of Agatha Christie have been read by millions of people.
10 He was brought up by monkeys in the jungle.

2 Grammar

1 had cleaned   2 have redecorated   3 has cut
4 having serviced   5 had taken out   6 have mended
7 have cooked   8 have tested   9 had repaired
10 have made

3 Vocabulary

1 B   2 D   3 B   4 D   5 A   6 B   7 C   8 A   9 C   10 D

4 Word formation

1 painter   2 paintings   3 architecture
4 scientist   5 writer   6 mathematicians
7 astronomer   8 archaeologist   9 sculptor
10 building

5 Vocabulary *

1 They can't have children so they want to adopt a little girl.
2 People come up to me in the street and ask me the time.
3 When did you realize your purse was missing?
4 Be quiet ! You chatter like monkeys!
5 The shock was so great that it left me speechless.
6 Cities are not good places to bring up children.
7 A new hairstyle will transform your appearance.
8 Please translate this into English.
9 We caught a shoal of fish.
10 The factory will employ more people next year.

Progress test 11

1 Grammar

1 People who come from Holland are Dutch.
2 Bob Marley, who wrote many hit songs, was Jamaican.
3 The Smiths, who arrived late, missed the bus.
4 The book which I've just read is about Harry Potter.
5 Leonardo DiCaprio, whose mother is German, was born in Hollywood.
6 This song, which is on their latest CD, is their best song ever.
This song, which is their best song ever, is on their latest CD.
7 Scotland, which has a lot of snow, is part of the United Kingdom.
8 Buffalo Bill, whose real name was William Cody, was a buffalo hunter.
9 Mother Teresa, who was born in Albania, went to help the poor in India.
Mother Teresa, who went to help the poor in India, was born in Albania.
10 Calcutta, which has a lot of poor people, is the capital of West Bengal.
Calcutta, which is the capital of West Bengal, has a lot of poor people.

2 Grammar

1 when   2 whose   3 who
4 who   5 where   6 whose
7 where   8 when   9 which
10 who

3 Vocabulary

1 ✗   2 ✗   3 ✗
4 the   5 ✗   6 the
7 the   8 ✗   9 ✗
10 ✗

4 Vocabulary

1 musician	2 millionaire	3 terrorists
4 celebrity	5 murderer	6 politicians
7 dictator	8 favourite	9 leaders
10 blackmailer		

5 Vocabulary

1 slum	2 embassy	3 struggle
4 chairperson	5 ceremony	6 award
7 gangster	8 journalist	9 personality
10 democracy		

Progress test 12

1 Grammar

1 will have found	2 will be flying	3 will be lying
4 will have risen	5 will be working	6 will be watching
7 will still be going	8 will have finished	9 will be living
10 will be waiting		

2 Grammar

1 By twelve o'clock, I will have finished the shopping.
2 I will be getting our lunch ready at one o'clock.
3 In ten year's time, some wild animals will have become extinct.
4 Next week, we will be celebrating Easter.
5 They will have been working here for three years by May.
6 They won't be knocking down that old building until next year.
7 Robots will be doing our housework before the end of this century.
8 By next summer, she will have finished her studies.
9 Politicians will not have solved the problem of global warming until 2010.
10 By the end of this year, we will have played six football matches.

3 Grammar

1 B   2 A   3 C   4 D   5 D   6 C   7 A   8 C   9 D   10 B

4 Vocabulary

1 carry on	2 got away	3 set off
4 get back	5 find out	6 turned into
7 pick up	8 bring up	9 made up
10 got on		

5 Vocabulary *

1 Can you imitate the way other people speak?
2 The mental ability of robots is not very great.
3 I admit that I ate all of the biscuits.
4 The discotheque will create problems in this quiet little village.
5 Everyone in our family shares the household jobs like washing and cooking.
6 The problem is not that bad – you mustn't exaggerate.
7 An optimist thinks things are going to get better.
8 I like electronic gadgets such as computers and mobile phones.
9 Please don't say anything to embarrass me in front of all my friends.
10 I forgot to mention that there's a party on Saturday.

Progress test 13

1 Grammar

1 She told me she lived in an old house in the country.
2 She said she was living with her parents.
3 He said he had just finished school.
4 He told us he had played football the week before.
5 He told me he had been having a bath when the lights had gone out.
6 The weather man said it would be cold and wet the following/next day.
7 She said she had to go and have her hair done then.
8 She said that was the last warning she was going to give me/us.
9 She admitted she still hadn't read those books.
10 He said he would meet me/us there the following week at the same time.

2 Grammar

1 'I saw the robber leave the bank.' she said.
2 'Go to bed,' she told them.
3 'I couldn't get to sleep that night,' he said.
4 'I'll phone you tomorrow,' he told her.
5 'Can you phone me this evening?' she asked him
6 'We have to get up early tomorrow morning,' they said.
7 'We don't want to be late,' they said.
8 'I'm going into town later this morning,' she said.
9 'I've always wanted to play James Bond,' he told them.
10 'I was working at a tea company before I became a spy,' Pond said.

3 Vocabulary

1 C   2 D   3 A   4 B   5 D   6 A   7 C   8 B   9 D   10 A

4 Vocabulary

1 checked	2 haunted	3 delay
4 arrest/catch	5 commit	6 creak
7 arrive	8 case/suitcase/bag	9 Dangerous
10 mist		

5 Vocabulary *

1 The postman will deliver a big parcel to our house today.
2 The producer of the film said he could not spend any more money.
3 A doctor can earn more than a teacher.
4 The first scene of the film was very interesting.
5 Falling out of that window was an incredible stunt.
6 A strange noise came from the old house.
7 The police will charge him with the murder.
8 The empty hotel had a spooky atmosphere.
9 He tried to threaten them with a knife.
10 Fear of the dark is quite usual among children.

Progress test 14

1 Grammar

1 My aunt asked me if/whether I liked ice cream.
2 The man asked me where I was from.
3 My mum asked us why we didn't take up the piano.
4 She asked me if/whether I had ever been to Disneyland.
5 The teacher asked me when I had last been/gone to the dentist.
6 The woman asked us if/whether we could speak any other languages.
7 I asked the girl if/whether she had to leave so soon.
8 She asked me if/whether we would see some paintings by Picasso.
9 He asked her why she wore jeans all the time.
10 She asked me if/whether I had enjoyed the film.

2 Grammar

1 Could you tell me the way to the railway station?
2 Would you mind telling her why you took her book?
3 Can you tell me if you know who painted that picture?
4 Do you know where Endelberg comes from?
5 Have you any idea what the time is?
6 Can you tell me how to get to the post office?
7 Could you tell me how much a stamp to England costs?
8 Do you know the name of the man who painted *Guernica*?
9 Would you mind telling me how much you earn?
10 Have you any idea how much this painting is worth?

3 Error correction

| 1 been to | 2 worried about | 3 suceed in |
| 4 looking forward to | 5 taken part in | |

4 Vocabulary

1 in	2 about	3 on
4 of	5 about	6 of
7 for	8 of	9 at
10 about		

5 Vocabulary *

1. I haven't read the book, but I've just had a quick glance at it.
2. She was dressed in black.
3. I need to get to know her before I can say whether I like her.
4. Well-known artists get a lot of work.
5. The witness drew a sketch of the man who had robbed the bank.
6. Let's explore the island as it's our first visit.
7. She was very popular because of her cheerful nature.
8. The rooms at the back of the house are dark and gloomy.
9. That portrait of John doesn't look much like him.
10. She is very sincere and always says exactly what she feels.

Progress test 15

1 Grammar

1 in case	2 as soon as	3 before
4 after	5 while	6 by the time
7 until	8 as soon as	9 Once
10 when		

2 Grammar

1 agreed	2 made	3 avoid
4 can't stand	5 should	6 refused
7 managed	8 denied	9 you'd better
10 enjoy		

3 Vocabulary

1 in	2 about	3 for
4 of	5 to	6 in
7 about	8 to	9 to
10 against		

4 Vocabulary

1 bear	2 giraffe	3 whale
4 camel	5 swallow	6 zebra
7 shark	8 mosquito	9 elephant
10 dove		

5 Vocabulary *

1. Monarch butterflies face extinction if we don't do something to save them.
2. She was lucky to survive the accident.
3. Birds flap their wings when they fly.
4. Do you have a calendar so that we can check the date of the concert?
5. Scientists are carrying out an experiment with plants.
6. Swallows migrate south every winter.
7. He tried to persuade her to lend him money.
8. You can't convince me that you're telling the truth.
9. We are responsible for the state of the environment.
10. As the ship sailed closer, the island appeared on the horizon.

Term test 1 (Units 1–5)

1 Grammar

1 goes	2 am washing	3 started
4 have lived	5 have been reading	6 have just finished
7 had already started	8 was raining	9 hated
10 would always forget		

2 Grammar

1 have never been	2 catch	3 am reading
4 used to speak	5 would go	6 have been waiting
7 hadn't seen	8 was washing	9 had been working
10 owned		

3 Grammar

1 D   2 C   3 B   4 A   5 C   6 A   7 D   8 B   9 B   10 C

4 Vocabulary

1 nervous	2 shy	3 ambitious
4 expensive	5 intelligent	6 dull
7 stubborn	8 funny	9 pessimistic
10 confident		

5 Word formation

1 impatient	2 successful	3 attractions
4 exciting	5 practical	6 aggressive
7 unusual	8 seriously	9 generous
10 curious		

6 Vocabulary

1 package	2 night	3 pen
4 concert	5 platform	6 return
7 crew	8 flight/plane	9 by
10 casual/informal		

Term test 2 (Units 6–10)

1 Grammar

1 A   2 B   3 C   4 D   5 D   6 B   7 D   8 C   9 A   10 C

2 Key word transformations

1. If you had arrived sooner, you would have caught the bus.
2. If I had a car, I would need a driving licence.
3. The Smith's house was broken into while they were on holiday.
4. The new block of flats will be finished next year.
5. Their car is being repaired at the moment.
6. You need to have your flat redecorated.
7. She wouldn't have married him if she had not wanted to have a family.
8. I wish we hadn't missed the concert.
9. If only I had spoken to you on the phone!
10. You don't need to have your hair cut.

3 Grammar

1 can	2 must	3 should
4 can't	5 must	6 might
7 shouldn't	8 can't	9 needn't
10 can't		

4 Word formation

1 disadvantages	2 behaviour	3 forgotten
4 noisy	5 unhealthy	6 disagree
7 discovery	8 predictions	9 global
10 tropical		

5 Vocabulary

1 had	2 go	3 do
4 get	5 flock	6 pile
7 set	8 make	9 Take
10 do		

6 Vocabulary

1 endangered	2 chat	3 colleague
4 bark	5 root	6 staff
7 attend	8 herd	9 realize
10 traffic		

Term test 3 (Units 11–15)

1 Grammar

1 She's the girl who won the prize.
2 That's the man whose wallet I found.
3 These are the things which I want you to buy.
4 This is the present which my friend gave me for Christmas.
5 That's the church where they got married.
6 It was 1999 when I met her.
7 People who are interested in politics sometimes become politicians.
8 Slums, which exist in many cities, are a problem.
9 They go to the seaside where they sunbathe all day.
10 Those are the friends whose football I borrowed.

2 Grammar

1 driving	2 get	3 to do
4 to obey	5 going	6 listening
7 doing	8 ring	9 to tell
10 asking		

3 Error correction

1 I arrive	2 would let	3 will be living
4 had never been	5 will have moved	6 leaves
7 know	8 had to	9 could
10 was living		

4 Vocabulary

1 ✗	2 an	3 ✗
4 ✗	5 a	6 ✗
7 the	8 ✗	9 the
10 ✗		

5 Vocabulary

1 C   2 D   3 A   4 D   5 C   6 A   7 A   8 D   9 D   10 B

6 Word formation

1 imitation	2 optimistic	3 producer
4 murderer	5 musician	6 favourite
7 embarrassing	8 investigation	9 able
10 survival		

Final test (Units 1–15)

1 Grammar

1 do you do	2 am writing	3 met
4 have dropped	5 had already cooked	6 were you doing
7 have never seen	8 had been studying	9 has been waiting
10 didn't use	11 will see	12 will be going
13 is going to snow	14 will have finished	15 am going to have
16 was assassinated	17 are having	18 find
19 didn't have	20 hadn't found	

2 Key word transformations

1 She told them she had never seen such a beautiful garden before.
2 She wondered if/whether they could give her some information about the concert.
3 She asked if/whether they knew the way to the railway station.
4 She wanted to know when he had started to cook.
5 He was pleased when he was picked up at the airport.
6 You'd better have your roof repaired.
7 She would not have lost her purse if she had closed her bag.
8 I wish I had gone to bed earlier before the exam.
9 She has been taking French lessons for five years.
10 I used to live in an old house but now I live in a flat.

3 Vocabulary

1 D	2 B	3 C
4 B	5 A	6 C
7 B	8 C	9 D
10 C	11 B	12 B
13 A	14 A	15 B
16 D	17 B	18 D
19 A	20 D	

4 Vocabulary

1 set	2 fell	3 case
4 better	5 to	6 for
7 gone	8 soon	9 to
10 up	11 wish	12 could
13 set	14 most	15 swarm
16 in	17 part	18 brought
19 had	20 checked	

5 Vocabulary

1 cheap	2 neat	3 tight
4 pilot	5 return	6 deck
7 revise	8 education	9 predict
10 astronomer		

6 Word formation

1 expensive	2 patient	3 ambitious
4 enthusiasm	5 confidence	6 impolite
7 recently	8 disappeared	9 unsuccessfully
10 politician		

7 Writing *

Dear Sir or Madam,

I am writing in reply to your advertisement for young people to take part in the TV quiz show: 'Genius'.
I am 13 years old and I attend the Central School in Birmingham. First of all, I would like to say that I usually get good results in tests especially in science subjects: I am one of the top five students in the class.
I also think I have a good voice because our teacher has asked me to read a poem at the annual Literature and Music Festival which is held at our school.
I would like to appear on the show because I enjoy answering general knowledge questions. Moreover, I have never been inside a TV studio and I am curious to know what it is like.
Finally, if I won any money on the show, I would use it to go on holiday with my parents, who haven't had a holiday for a long time.

I hope my application will be successful.

I look forward to hearing from you,

Yours faithfully,